Elite • 248

Post-Roman Kingdoms

'Dark Ages' Gaul & Britain, AD 450–800

**RAFFAELE D'AMATO &
ANDREA SALIMBETI**

ILLUSTRATED BY ANDREI NEGIN
Series editors Martin Windrow & Nick Reynolds

Print ISBN: 978 1 4728 5098 0
ePub: 978 1 4728 5094 2
ePDF: 978 1 4728 5091 1
XML: 978 1 4728 5093 5

Editor: Martin Windrow
Index by Alan Rutter
Typeset by PDQ Digital Media Solutions, Bungay, UK
Printed and bound in India by Replika Press Private Ltd.

Dedication

To the Celts still living today throughout the world, in remembrance of
their roots and their glorious past.

Acknowledgements

Assembling the information and illustrations for this complex subject,
particularly in times of widespread disruption due to the pandemic, has
required our seeking advice and assistance from many friends, colleagues,
museums and other institutions. While the constraints of space prevent us
from detailing here their individual contributions, all of those listed below
have earned the authors' sincere gratitude for their patience and generosity
in sharing their expertise and resources.

In Britain, old and new friends put their resources at our disposal: Brett
Hammond, Chris Wren and the library of Timeline Auctions, Stephen
Pollington, Matt Bunker, and Dan Shadrake of the group 'Britannia'. Despite
the difficulties faced by the staffs of museums closed during the pandemic,
many have found ways to provide us with valuable cooperation, and access
to little-known material. We wish to express our gratitude to Dr Angie
Bolton, curator of the Oxfordshire Museum; Dr Clare McNamara of the
National Museum of Ireland; to the National Museum of Wales, in the
persons of Drs Mark Lewis, Mark Redknap, and Sian Iles; and to Drs Lydia
Prosser, Martin Goldberg and Margaret Wilson of the National Museum of
Scotland.

In Brittany, Benjamin Franckaert and the group 'Letavia' were helpful in
many ways. For material on important archaeological specimens, we
express our warm thanks to Dr Six Manon and M Alain Amet of the Musée
de Bretagne; to Dr Guénolé Ridoux and Prof Bernard Hulin for important
material from Landevennec; and, for precious information from the Ruscino
depot in Languedoc-Roussillon, to Dr Laurent Savarese and Dr Elisabeth
Doumeyrou (Direction du patrimoine historique et de l'archéologie, ville de
Perpignan), and to Prof Michael Feugère.

Great thanks are due to Giovanni Scorcioni, for access to a facsimile copy of
the *Vergilius Romanus* codex (of which the original is preserved in the
Vatican Library). This allows us to publish important military images from
what is believed to be the earliest British illuminated manuscript.

Photographic sources to which we owe gratitude include the following
museums and institutions: the Portable Antiquity Scheme (PAS); Norwich
Castle Museum & Art Gallery; the British Museum; Timeline Auctions;
Ruthwell Parish; Govan Old Parish Church Museum; the Koninklijke Musea
voor Kunst en Geschiedenis in Brussels; the Bibliothèque Nationale de
France; the Musée Départemental Arles Antique in Arles ; the Musée de
Dauphinois in Grenoble; the Musée Gallo-Romain de Lyon-Fourvière; the
Deutsches Historisches Museum, Berlin; and the New York Metropolitan
Museum.

The graphic and computer preparation of images is the result of the hard
work of Dr Marco Saliola, to whom the authors are deeply indebted. The
hypothetical reconstructions in the colour plates were particularly
challenging, and only the knowledge and talent of Dr Prof Andrei Negin
could have brought them to life; for his hard work, and his patience
(especially with one of the authors), we acknowledge our great gratitude.
Raffaele D'Amato
Andrea Salimbeti

Title page photograph
'Battle between Latins and Trojans', a miniature from folio 188v of the
Vergilius Romanus codex, 5th–6th century. Details include both 'Phrygian'
caps and crested helmets; iron scale *loricae* with sleeves and skirt edged
with yellow metal; and a recurved composite bow, plus a striped quiver on
the ground. (facsimile, Cod. Vat. lat. 3867; photo Raffaele D'Amato)

CONTENTS

'DARK AGES' GAUL & BRITAIN, AD 450–800

INTRODUCTION

A well-preserved post-Roman *Spangenhelm* dated to AD 480–524, from Vézeronce, Isère, south-eastern France. Produced in Eastern Roman workshops, it is an example of a type used by the Gallo-Roman elite during the second half of the 5th century and first half of the 6th. (Grenoble, Musée de Dauphinois; photo ex D'Amato & Negin, courtesy of the Museum)

Sub-Roman and post-Roman

In the popular imagination, the sack of Rome by Alaric's Visigoths in AD 410 marked the end of Roman civilization in the West, and the rise of Germanic 'barbarian' kingdoms amid the ashes of the Late Roman world. In fact, of course, this transition was a process rather than an event, which lasted from the early 5th into at least the 7th century. The Emperor Honorius continued to reign until his death in 423 (though from 418 he was obliged to cede lands in southern Gaul to the Visigoths, in return for their help against the Vandals and Alans). Roman culture survived stubbornly in various territories, and even in some autonomous polities, defended by Imperially-appointed *patricii* ('patricians' – a title of political authority) and generals.

Even after the final extinction of the Western Empire in 476, in both Gaul and Britain the local 'afterlife' of Roman law, institutions and material culture was lengthy, and included the development of military organizations drawing on Roman and Celtic traditions alike. Consequently, in many cases the term 'sub-Roman' was for several generations more appropriate than simply 'post-Roman'. Neither were the Romano-Celtic defenders or the Germanic incomers unified power-blocks. From at least the 4th century many Germanic warriors had served the Empire as army recruits or as employed 'allies', and during the constant wars of the so-called 'Dark Ages' rival leaders among each cultural group pursued competitive struggles. Alliances might also be formed across ethnic lines: for instance, in 451, by the Western *Magister Utriusque Militiae* (supreme commander) Aetius with the Visigothic king Theodoric I against Attila's Huns, and again in the 460s between Aetius and Childeric of the northern Franks against the Visigoths. For centuries, the ethnic make-up of many armed forces continued to be mixed.

In Britain, a 'Celtic revival' during the 5th and 6th centuries, between the end of centralized Imperial

Images of Late Roman statuette of cavalryman, *c.* AD 400, from Yorkshire. Measuring 4.5cm (1¾ ins) long, it represents a Romano-British rider wearing a 'Phrygian' cap and a cloak, and carrying a small round shield. (PAS YORYM-C2A231, Creative Commons Licence CC BY4.0)

rule and the establishment of the early Anglo-Saxon kingdoms, saw Romano-British peoples reverting to local government based on former tribal entities 'which still aspired to Roman ideals, rather than [having] a conscious desire to return to a pre-Roman Celtic past'. According to Kenneth Dark, the Late Roman Christian heritage in Britain was maintained at least into the 7th century. The language was still a local form of late Latin spoken alongside Brittonic languages, and these peoples called themselves *Cymry* (from *combrogi*, 'fellow countrymen') in common identification with their former status as Roman citizens. The term has been preserved in *Cymru*, the Welsh-language name for modern Wales, and both the Saxons and the Franks called the Romano-Britons *Wealas* or 'Welsh'.

Even within the territories controlled by Germanic suzerains, some Gallo-Romans enjoyed a certain degree of independence thanks to the work of the Church. Sub-Roman Gauls strove to maintain the orthodox Catholic faith against the Arian heresy followed by the Visigoths, and Roman civilisation against barbarism, at least until Clovis I, first king of the united Franks, accepted Catholic conversion in the last years of the 5th century.[1] It has even been argued that developments in the former territories of the Roman West were 'not so much the Germanisation of the Romans, as the Romanisation of the Germans'. The courage and skills of the ancient Bretons of Armorica (north-western France, between the rivers Loire and Seine) allowed them to preserve, by both arms and diplomacy, a *de facto* autonomy until at least the late 8th century.

Sources
In researching the historical background of the sub-Roman Celtic lands, the scarce archaeology (especially in Britain)

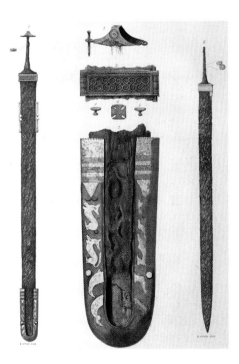

Late Roman *spatha* swords, 5th century, from Brighthampton, Oxfordshire, with decoration in mixed Germanic and Romano-Celtic styles. (Left) Sword from Grave 31. (Centre) Details from Grave 31: copper-alloy pommel; stamped and engraved decoration on guard, apparently of base silver; two of four copper-alloy studs, and a small silver cross, found near the guard; scabbard chape. (Right) Sword from Grave 44. (ex-Akerman, 1860)

1 In this text, 'Catholic' or 'orthodox' indicates adherence to the Nicene Creed, first adopted in AD 325 and confirmed in 383.

'The hunting of Julo', a miniature from folio 163r of the *Vergilius Romanus* codex dated to the 5th–6th century. Note Phrygian-style caps, *tunica manicata* decorated with *clavi* and *orbiculi*, close-fitting trousers patterned with horizontal stripes, and ankle-boots. The weapons are long *hasta* spears and a recurved composite bow. (facsimile, Cod. Vat. lat. 3867; photo Raffaele D'Amato)

and iconography are supported by later-written sources of many kinds. Apart from the early 6th-century work of Gildas, and Bede's 8th-century *Ecclesiastical History*, Nennius's *Historia Brittonum*, the *Anglo-Saxon Chronicles*, the *Annales Cambriae*, the *Y Gododdin*, *Chulch & Olwen* by Neirin ('Aneirin'), Taliesin's tales, and the *Mabinogion* were only written down between the 9th and 12th centuries, as was Geoffrey of Monmouth's epic pseudo-history *Historiae Regum Britanniae*. (See the beginning of the Select Bibliography on page 56 for abbreviations of such sources quoted in textual references.) But while the transcriptions from an oral bardic tradition dating from earlier centuries must certainly be approached with great caution, they do include references relevant to the period of sub-Roman Britain – for instance, some descriptions of arms and armours find echoes in archaeological finds. As in the case of the *Iliad*, the preserved words of bards may be those used in their own lifetimes, but they also describe real elements of earlier periods.

Again, although the earliest surviving manuscript of the poem (Cardiff MS 2.81) is usually dated to the mid-13th century, *Y Gododdin* mentions 'Arthur' (YG XXXIII, in the archaic version). This source is believed to date from the 590s, being transmitted orally before its transcription perhaps in the 9th–10th century. His mention in 6th – 7th-century oral tradition argues for Arthur's historical existence – perhaps as an appointed sub-Roman *Dux Bellorum* who unified a part of Britain, or simply as a strong and mobile Romano-British warlord who succeeded in keeping the Germanic advances in check for a number of years. Across the Channel, more concrete historical sources help give us a relatively clear picture of the last Gallo-Romans in Brittany, central and southern France before the age of Charlemagne.

A

PATRICII ARMIES; GAUL, 5th–6th CENTURY
(1) *Magister Militum* and *Patricius*, AD 460–480

According to his brother-in-law Sidonius Apollinaris, the *Patricius* Ecdicius Avitus wore a helmet with cheek-guards, a ringmail *lorica*, and greaves. In accordance with his rank, we have given him the splendid gilded *Spangenhelm* from Vézeronce, and a *lorica* edged with copper-alloy or gilded rings. His *spatha* and *semispatha* are copied from examples found in the grave of the allied Frankish king Childeric, both being products of Byzantine workshops. The whole equipment follows Late Roman models, and is worn over a padded undergarment with *pteryges* at the upper arms, over a utilitarian tunic and trousers. The warrior from his retinue **(2)** carries his general's purple cloak, with its gilt 'crossbow' *fibula* at the shoulder. His spear and shield are held by a *famulus* or servant in his military household **(3)**, and are reconstructed from finds at Cutry and Rhenen respectively. Colours in this plate are from miniatures in the *Vergilius Romanus* codex.

(2) *Laetus*, c.450–510

This Germanic volunteer soldier's defensive equipment is again wholly Late Roman, with the *Bandenhelm* from Bretzenheim, a moulded leather *lorica,* and copper-alloy greaves. The magnificent sword is from the Kemathen specimen, as reconstructed by A. Strassmeir. Other details are copied from grave-finds at Julich, which show the use of composite belts with copper-alloy fittings. Note his *sagum* cloak fastened by a silver-gilt brooch from Trier, and the *francisca* axe that he carries.

(3, 3) *Famuli* military servants, mid-5th century

The long-sleeved tunic remained the basic garment among the Gallo-Romans, usually of wool or linen but sometimes of imported Egyptian cotton or oriental silk. Since the 3rd century the *tunica militaris* had increasingly been decorated, with vertical *clavi* stripes from the shoulders, with neck and cuff stripes, skirt borders, and with patterned patches applied to the shoulders and skirt – either circular (*orbiculi*) or of other shapes (*segmenta*). Trousers might be long and close-fitting or short below the knee, with or without wrapped 'puttees' or shaped leggings. Waist belts might be ornamented in various fashions (SA, *Ep.*, IV. ix. 2). The standing man also wears a hooded over-garment; variations might be a cape-length *alicula*, or this longer *cucullus* of Gallic origin. This man's appearance probably represents that of the simple infantry, armed with spears, long knives (*cultra venatoria*) and/or a *francisca* throwing-axe, and carrying a shield if available.

SELECT CHRONOLOGY (AD)

Note: Many dates and entries, particularly for Britain, are speculative, being compiled from debatable and conflicting later sources including pseudo-historical poetic works. Personal names survive in varying forms from different languages, and many place-names are not identifiable with modern sites. References transition from 'Romano-British' to the Anglo-Saxon term 'Welsh'.

5th century:

407–410 'Official' end of Roman rule in Britain, as usurper F. Claudius Constantinus withdraws regular garrisons to the continent; Emperor Honorius sends the 'Honorian rescript' telling the Britons to look to their own defence.

c.423–475 *Prolonged defence of Gaul by Magister Militum Flavius Aetius (c.391–454) and his lieutenants and successors Litorius (d. 439), Aegidius (fl.458–464), and Ecdicius Avitus (c.420–c.475). These generals sometimes form temporary alliances with individual Germanic kings.*

429 In Britain, 'battle of the Alleluia'; Germanus of Auxerre leads Romano-Britons to victory over Saxons and Picts (Pauli Diaconi, *Historia Romana*, XIV,14).

c.446–448 'The Groan of the Britons': British appeal to Aetius for help against the Picts.
Some Gallo-Romans gain practical independence, nominally as *foederati* ('allies') of the Empire.

447–448 South-eastern British ruler Vortigern (Wyrtgeorn/Gwrtheyrn) summons help from Jutish (Saxon) leaders Hengist and Horsa (ACd9.1).

c.450–455? Saxons seize more territory in Kent. Vortimer, son of Vortigern, wins four victories over them; Horsa is killed at battle of Aegelsthrep.

450 St Patrick reprimands king Ceretic of Strathclyde for attacking Irish Christian converts.

451 In Gaul, battle of 'Catalaunian Field' near Châlons or Troyes. Aetius, with Visigothic king Theodoric I and other Germanic allies, defeats Huns under Attila.

454 Death of Aetius.

456 Four companies of Britons are defeated at Crecganford; Romano-Britons give up Kent and fall back on London.

458 In Gaul, Aegidius, appointed *Magister Militum per Gallias* by Emperor Majorian (r. 457–461), defeats Visigoths under Theodoric II at Arelate (Arles), and recaptures Lyons from the Burgundians (northern Franks).

c.460 While attending a peace-banquet, many Romano-British leaders are treacherously killed by Saxon hosts. Captured, Vortigern is forced to cede territories in modern Essex, Middlesex and Sussex.

461–464 Aegidius now lacks Imperial authority but remains active, defeating Visigoths at Orléans (463) in alliance with Childeric, king of the northern Franks (Hydatius p.117; *Gallic Chronicle*).

464 On death of Aegidius, his son Syagrius inherits Gallo-Roman 'kingdom' around Soissons. In alliance with Childeric, he drives Saxons off islands in the Loire between Saumur and Angers.

469/470 Sidonius Apollinaris named bishop of Clermont. Riothamus, *Dux of Britanni*, is defeated by Visigoths near Châteauroux. *Comes* Paulus, with both Roman and Frankish troops, plunders the Goths, but is then killed.

473 Saxon victories over Romano-Britons, winning great spoils. Some scholars date to about this time a battle at Wallop (Hampshire) between Romano-British war-leader Ambrosius and Vortigern's dynasty.

474   In Gaul, Ecdicius Avitus of Auvergne is appointed *Magister Militum* and *Patricius* by Emperor Julius Nepos (SA, *Ep.* V, 16).

475–477   Visigoths conquer and are ceded last Roman territories in the Auvergne. Germanic general Odoacer declares himself king of Italy, thus ending Western Empire but recognizing authority of Eastern Roman emperor, Zeno. In Britain, Saxon king Aelle lands at Cymensora (?) on Channel coast; Saxons kill many 'Welsh' (Britons), driving others north into the Weald.

485   Aelle fights the Welsh near Merecredesburnan (Binsted, Sussex?).

486   Battle of Soissons; Clovis's Franks defeat Syagrius and conquer his 'kingdom'.

491   Saxons conquer Pevensey and massacre Britons.

493   Battle of Bown Hill in Severn valley; Ambrosius's final campaign against the Saxons (PDHR, XV, 19)

495   Saxon Cerdic and his son Cynric land at Cerdicesora (?) on south-west British coast. Rebellions by Anglo-Saxon mercenaries against Romano-Britons.

6th century:

c.490–515?   *According to Nennius, Romano-British led by the* Dux Bellorum Artorius *(Arthur) inflict twelve defeats on Saxons, culminating at Mount Badon (Liddington Castle/ Eorthbyrig ?, Wiltshire).*

495–540   *Vortiporius rules as high king (protictor) of Dyfed.*

507   In Gaul, Apollinaris, son of Sidonius, leads nobles of the Auvergne alongside Alaric II's Visigoths against Clovis's Franks at battle of Vouillé near Poitou. Alaric is killed, as are many Auvergnat aristocrats. (HF, II, 37)

508/519?   Saxons under Cerdic defeat with great slaughter Britons led by Natanlaod, at Natanleag (Netley, Hampshire?), and found kingdom of Wessex.

514   Another Saxon victory at Cerdicesora?.

527   Battle between South Saxons and Britons at Cerdiceslea (?).

530   Saxons conquer Isle of Wight and massacre Britons.

[535–c.550?]   *Extreme global weather events, causing famine and plague throughout NW Europe.]*

537/543?   According to *Annales Cambriae* (B546.1), battle of Camlann; Arthur is killed or fatally wounded during a civil war.

540/560?   In Gaul, Conomor (Marcus Cuonomorius, perhaps Mark of Cornwall?), *Comes* of Carhaix, *Praefectus Francorum Regis* and ruler of both Cornwall and Brittany, is defeated and killed by his stepson Judael with help of Frankish king Clothar.

552   Saxon victory over Britons at Salisbury, Wiltshire.

556   Saxon victory at Beran Byrg (Barbury, Wiltshire?).

571   Saxon victory at Biedanford (Bedford).

573   Battle of Arderydd, Cumbria; Gwendolleu ap Ceidio, king of Arderydd, defeated and killed either by brothers Peredur and Gwrgi, or by Ridderch Hael, king of Strathclyde (ACb601.1–602.2).

577   Battle of Deorham (?); West Saxons under Ceawlin defeat Britons under *reges* Conmail, Farinmail and Condidan. Fall of Bath, Cirencester and Gloucester to Saxons.

584   Battle of Fethanleag (Stoke Lyne, Oxfordshire?); West Saxon king Cutha, son of Cuthwine, is defeated and killed by Britons.

578–590   *In northern Gaul, wars between the Bretons (Brittani) under*

Waroch (Gwereg) II and the Franks under Chilperic I and Guntram (HF, V, 26, 29).

597 Northumbrian Saxons defeat the British Gododdin of modern north-east England/south-east Scotland at Catraeth (Catterick, Yorkshire).

7th century:

614 Saxon victory at Beandun (Badbury, Dorset?).

616 Battle of Chester; Saxon king Aethelferth slaughters British forces of Selyf Sargaffgadau of Powys and Cadwal Crysban of Gwynedd, and kills 1,200 monks (HE, II, 2).

631–633 Cadwallon of Gwynedd defeats Anglo-Saxons of Deira and Bernicia at battle of Meicen (Hatfield Chase, Yorkshire?), killing king Edwin and his sons. Allied with Penda of Mercia, Cadwallon ravages Northumbria and occupies it for a year (HE, II, 20-III,1).

634 Cadwallon defeated and killed by Oswald, king of Bernicia, at Catscaul (Heavenfield, near Hexham?; HE, III, 1, 2).

635 Judicael of Brittany wins two battles against Franks before signing a peace with king Dagobert.

642 Penda of Mercia and allies are defeated by Oswald of Bernicia at Maes Cogwy (Oswestry, Shropshire?).

652–654 Battles between Britons and Saxons at Bradford-on-Avon (?) and elsewhere; death of Cyndyllan of Powys, ally of Mercia.

658 West Saxon victory over the Welsh at Penselwood.

665 Second battle of Badon, between northern Welsh and Mercians against Northumbrian Saxons.

682 Centwine's West Saxons win victory over the Welsh.

8th century:

710 Geraint, king of Cornwall, is killed by West Saxons at battle of Llongborth (Langport, Somerset?).

720–722 Victories by Cornish Britons over West Saxons at Hehil, Garth Maelog and Pencon (?).

728–735 Welsh victories at Carno Mountain, and Saxon victory at Devawdan (?).

744–757 *Wars between Strathclyde and the Picts, and Cuthred and later Cynewulf of Wessex against the Welsh.*
Welsh victories over Saxons at Marchan Wood and Hereford; Cynan Tindaethwy becomes king of all Wales.

748–799 *In Gaul, prolonged wars between Armorican duchies and Carolingian Franks.*

753 Pepin III the Short (son of Charles Martel, father of Charlemagne, and first Carolingian king of the Franks) conquers Vannes, south-west Brittany.

756–780 *In Britain, annals record the capture of Alt Clut (Strathclyde) by Pictish king Oengus; and successful expeditions by Welsh of Gwent and Glamorgan into Mercia.*

784 Mercia is devastated by the Welsh.

796 Battle of Rhuddlan; victory of Offa of Mercia over Welsh king Caradog ap Meiron.

POST-ROMAN GAUL

Historical background:
The *Patricii*

In AD 395 the Roman Empire was administratively divided into Western and Eastern halves, ruled by the sons of the Emperor Theodosius. From his court at Ravenna, Italy, Honorius reigned over the West (though ceding various Gallic territories to Germanic kings) until his death in 423.

Although local authority was officially exercised by Imperially-appointed *patricii* ('patricians'), and the troops – of mixed origins – in each area were commanded by a *magister militum* ('military master', general), in practice the rigid Late Roman social hierarchy in northern Gaul was beginning to collapse by the turn of the 4th/5th century. The effective Imperial presence progressively withdrew; wealthy landowners fled south to more stable areas, leaving surviving estates vying for leadership, while both local Gallo-Roman leaders and Germanic settlers – mainly Franks and Visigoths – established themselves in power. Some of the incomers were resisted, but most were recognized by the residual Roman authorities as 'allies'.

After the death of the *Patricius* Aegidius in 464, the Visigothic king Euric sought to extend his authority throughout Gaul. In the absence of effective Imperial forces (despite crushing taxation to pay for them), this was resisted by the Christian Church and by elements of the local Gallo-Roman elite. One source who was doubly qualified for these roles was Sidonius Apollinaris, an aristocrat who was appointed bishop of Clermont. Sidonius helped to organize resistance, as did his brother-in-law Ecdicius Avitus in his native Auvergne. Euric was also prevented from extending his conquests north of the Loire by the Roman *Comes* (count) Paulus, together with Frankish allies. After the death of Paulus, Syagrius, a son of Aegidius, inherited a sizeable sub-Roman 'kingdom' around Soissons, initially without Frankish resistance.

The Auvergne, the most loyal district which remained to the Empire in Gaul, was exposed for several years to Visigothic attacks, culminating in a siege of the city of Clermont, which put up a tenacious defence under Sidonius's leadership, assisted by Burgundian Frankish allies. Despite this, in 475, in return for territory in Provence, the Imperial authorities ceded the Auvergne to Euric's rule, though extracting a promise of religious tolerance from the Arian heretic king. The *Dux* (duke) Victorius, a Catholic Gallo-Roman, became *Comes* of Clermont, ruling the Auvergne in Euric's name (HF, II, 20).

Euric's death in 484 opened the way for the final subjection of Gaul under a single Germanic people. Under the leadership of Clovis I, the Franks soon advanced between the Somme and the Loire, and at Soissons in 486 Clovis defeated Syagrius, whom he subsequently executed, and conquered his

'Turnus and Iris': miniature from folio 74v of the *Vergilius Romanus* codex, 5th–6th century. At left, Turnus is shown in full Late Roman equipment: a gilded helmet with a red crest, cheek-guards, but no nasal guard; a silvered *squama* scale armour including the upper arms, with a row of gilded scales at the bottom edges; a round convex shield with a pronounced conical boss, and a spear or javelin. His tunic is decorated at the cuffs and bottom edge, and is worn with long close-fitting trousers, *calcei* ankle-boots, and a *sagum* fastened on the right shoulder with an annular brooch. Again, note striped quiver of arrows. (facsimile; photo Raffaele D'Amato)

Two images of the Gallo-Roman belt and buckle from the tomb of St Caesarius, 6th century. The ornate ivory buckle-plate depicts sleeping soldiers at Christ's sepulchre. (Musée Départemental Arles Antique; photos Raffaele D'Amato, courtesy of the Museum)

territory. In 507 Apollinaris, son of Sidonius, led the nobles of the Auvergne alongside Alaric II's Visigoths against Clovis's Franks at the battle of Vouillé near Poitou, in which the Visigoths were defeated and their king was killed – and also, according to Gregory of Tours, at a bloody cost to the Auvergnat aristocracy (HF, II, 37). Having thus defeated both his Germanic enemies and the last representatives of Roman power, Clovis and his Salian Frankish successors proceeded to unite most of Gaul under the rule of the Merovingian dynasty.

Armorica

The Armoricans inhabited north-western Gaul, between the rivers Loire in the south and Seine in the east (though Saxon raiders had also settled around both river-mouths), in the territories of later Brittany. Between the late 4th and early 7th century, many sub-Roman Britons migrated from modern England to Armorica, blending with the local people to form the later Bretons. All early medieval texts present the Bretons as a cohesive people whose origin-legend looked back to the British Isles, and *Britannus* was often used in the 5th century to denote an inhabitant of Armorica (EP, III. 9. 2; I.7.5).

According to Nennius, the first nucleus had been formed by troops of the Roman usurper Magnus Maximus, who in 383 defeated Gratian, and, 'unwilling to send back his warlike companions to their wives, children and possessions in Britain, conferred upon them numerous districts... These are the Armoric Britons, and they remain there to the present day' (HB 27).

However, it is rather from the 5th century that we find major British settlement in western Armorica; the reasons remain partially uncertain, but one was certainly the escape of Romano-Celtic populations from the Germanic invasions of Britain. At this time the Bretons, formally citizens of the Empire, fought alongside Imperial forces against the Germanic invaders. During the Visigothic expansion under Euric in *c.*470, the Bretons of

BRITTANY & ARMORICA, 5th–8th CENTURY
(1) *Loricatus* of Riothamus's army, *c.*AD 470
This Breton heavy cavalryman wears a ridge helmet of Iatrus-Krivina typology, which seems to be the main type represented in the *Vergilius Romanus* miniatures. We have given his mainly iron *squama* copper-alloy scales at the upper arms and abdomen; it is worn over a padded *globa* or *thoracomacus*. The *sagum* is fastened with a 'quoit brooch' from Sarre, Kent. His horse's harness is decorated in gold and almandine; though hidden here, a quiver for javelins would hang behind the saddle on the far side.

(2) *Draconarius, Arborychi*, early 6th century
The Germanic *Arborychi* guarding northern Gaul retained the Roman equipment and customs of their forefathers until the time of Procopius, *c.*550, when they were still recognized as 'belonging to the legions to which they were assigned when they served in ancient times, and they always carry their own standards when they enter battle, and always follow the customs of their fathers... They preserve the dress of the Romans in every particular, even as regards their shoes.' The *deigmata* on their shields were probably those of the units mentioned in the *Notitia Dignitatum* as defending the *Tractus Armoricanus* on the Loire, such as the *Mauri Osimiaci* represented here. This standard-bearer wears the *Bandenhelm* from Trévières, Normandy, as restored by Faider-Feytmans and France-Lanord with the bowl completely covered with leather, and a leather *lorica* reinforced with metal studs and fittings. His *draco* standard is taken from extensive Late Roman iconographic evidence.

(3) *Iud Armoricanus*, 778
This warrior is armed in the sub-Roman Dumnonic fashion traceable to south-west Britain, but his clothing and sword show a strong Carolingian influence. The helmet is of Praha-Stromovka type, probably originating in the Eastern Empire but attested by iconography in the Italian territories still under Roman control. '(A similar model is still visible on the head of Conan II, Duke of Brittany, in the 11th-century Bayeux Tapestry.) In the midst of battle such troops could resupply themselves with javelins, since carts filled with *lanceolae* accompanied the marching army.

ABOVE LEFT
Sub-Roman iron helmet,
c.475–510, from the Hainault
region of Belgium. The bowl
is reinforced with continuous
broad bands around the brow
and over the top from side to
side and front to back these
both flaring out sideways
at the bottom. The British
Museum's reconstruction of
the fragmentary Shorwell
helmet from the Isle of Wight
is basically similar. (Brussels;
Koninklijke Musea voor Kunst
en Geschiednis; photo Jona
Lindering, Universal Licence
CCO.1)

ABOVE RIGHT
Rusted iron fragments of
6th–7th century lamellar armour
from Ruscino in the Septimania
– the territory once forming
the western part of the Roman
province of *Gallia Narbonensis*,
around modern Carcassonne
and Béziers. (Photo courtesy of
Archaeological Depot, Ruscino)

Armorica marched to defend the territory north of the Loire under a leader named Riothamus. It is unclear what relationship they bore to the population of migrant Britons and native Armoricans. Riothamus may have been a ruler in Brittany, or merely the leader of a large war-band, perhaps at some time allied to Aegidius or Syagrius. When defending Berry with (reportedly) some 12,000 men, Riothamus was decisively defeated near Châteauroux and fled to the Burgundians with the remnant of his army. Later, according to some scholars, *Britanni* from Britannia fought alongside other Armoricans against the Frankish expansion under Clovis.

The language and culture of post-Roman Brittany were oriented towards south-west Britain. Isolated by language and culture from adjacent regions of Gaul now under Frankish control, Breton society evolved its own characteristic forms. The sea provided rapid communication between Brittany and Britain; in Britain itself new threats, territorial retreats, and partition between several separated hubs of resistance led to further waves of emigration to Armorica between the 5th and 8th centuries. Armorican resistance to Merovingian efforts to extend Frankish overlordship is evident from the work of Gregory of Tours, who provides our earliest evidence for an Armorican peninsula under the political control of local *comites*. Although there is no explicit evidence for Breton raids into Frankish lands in the mid-8th century, nevertheless the recalcitrance of this people is suggested by Charlemagne's subsequent organization of the border country in 778 under a single *praefectus:* Roland, of poetic fame.

The *Arborychi*

Procopius mentions this group in northern Gaul in the 5th century (*Wars*, XII, 9–19). According to his translator H.B. Dewing, they occupied the coast of modern Belgium and were probably Germanic Christian *foederati* of the Empire, who originally fought against the Franks but eventually recognized their authority. Procopius says that at the time of the Visigothic expansion 'it so happened that the Arborychi had become soldiers of the Romans. And the Germans [Visigoths], wishing to make this people subject to themselves... began to plunder their land ... But the Arborychi proved their valour and loyalty to the Romans... in this war, and since the [Visigoths] were not able to overcome them by force, they wished to win them over and make the two peoples kin by intermarriage.' Procopius relates that other Roman troops stationed on the frontiers of Gaul also yielded the territory they had been guarding, and went over, 'with their standards', to join the Arborychi and other Germans.

It is thought probable that the term Arborychi refers to troops in Gallo-Roman service defending the *Tractus Armoricanus*, i.e. the Roman army on the Loire. If the organization of Syagrius's army was primarily associated with the Late Roman military, then its composition would include significant numbers of men of Germanic origins, though possibly of Roman culture. Burials perhaps associated with his army are almost certainly those of a Germanic military élite in northern Gaul, some of whom may have become landowners at an early stage. Such evidence peters out from the mid-5th century, coinciding with the run-down of Imperial forces. Thereafter members of the old Gallo-Roman governing class increasingly accepted official positions under the new Frankish sovereigns, perhaps reconciled by the latters' conversion to the Catholic faith.

Two images of a shield boss *(umbo)* from Ruscino, 7th–8th century. The defenders of Ruscino, whether Roman or Germanic, were subjects of the Visigothic kingdom, and their equipment showed strong Germanic influences, following Gothic, Burgundian or other Frankish styles. (Photo courtesy of Archaeological Depot, Ruscino)

Southern Gaul

During the late 7th and early 8th century, modern Provence was formally subject to the Frankish Merovingian kings, but was in fact governed by its own regional nobility according to Roman, not Frankish law. Both Provence and Aquitaine enjoyed prestige and some autonomy, although this was threatened by the expansionist ambitions of Charles Martel (*c.*688–741), the powerful *majordomo* of the Frankish kings, who is famous for repelling invasions both by Saxons from the east and Arabs from the south.

MILITARY ORGANIZATION

Armies of the *Patricii*

The titles of *Magister Militum* and *Patricius* were given to commanders such as Aetius (*c.*391–454), Aegidius (*fl.*458–464), Ecdicius Avitus (*c.*420–post 475), and Syagrius (*c.*430–487?) – the latter being the last *Magister Militum per Gallias*, but styled by his Germanic enemies *Rex Romanorum*, 'King of the Romans'. Barbarian kings formally allied to the Empire also received such titles, e.g. Chilperic I of the Burgundians, *Magister Militum Galliarium* (SA, *Ep.*, V, 6; VII,17). Cities were under the command of *comites* (SA, *Ep.*,VII, 2). Each landowner had his personal military household retinue (*famuli*; SA, *Paneg.* VII, 251), like that led by Ecdicius against the Visigoths (SA, *Ep.* III. 3.3–8), which comprised 18 brave warriors (or 10, according to HF, II, 24). During the turmoil of the Germanic conquests Gallo-Roman militias were usually formed by local aristocratic landowners. Commanders and soldiers were called *duces* and *milites* respectively (SA, *Ep.*,VII, 7), but interestingly the soldiers were also called *paludati* (V,7), from a classical term for a military cloak. Other surviving archaic terms were *signifer* for a standard-bearer (III, 13), *praetoriani* for bodyguards, and *exercitus* for a gathered army.

A Gallic field army presumably still existed when Aegidius was appointed *Magister Militum per Gallias* in 457–458. Evidence for the survival of this

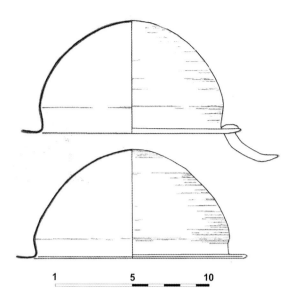

Drawings of two shield bosses from the Île Lavret, Brittany, variously dated between 650 and 920. These iron *umbones* were found placed over the chests of warriors in this group of burials, which also yielded two iron knives, a fragment of a sword blade, and a pair of iron spurs believed to be of late date. (Drawings by Andrea Salimbeti, ex Giot, 1988)

army into the 470s may also be inferred from Paul the Deacon (PDHR, XV, 4). Aegidius, both as *magister militum* and as an independent warlord, would have had his own *bucellarii*, probably (as was common) mainly barbarians. It is conceivable that, after Aegidius broke with the Imperial government in Italy in 461, the distinction between the remnants of the Gallic field army and Aegidius's increasingly numerous personal following became blurred. Aegidius may also have had access to other remnants of the military structure in northern Gaul, such as *limitanei* and *coloni*. The regions of *Belgica Prima* and *Secunda* had been areas of mercenary settlement from the 3rd century onwards, e.g. by the Sarmatians recorded in northern Gaul by the *Notitia Dignitatum*, and the Sarmatian and Alan presence in *Belgica II* east of Paris. These military settlements have been proposed as continuing sources of military manpower into the Merovingian period.

Aegidius, Syagrius, and the kings of the Salian Franks had common interests in resisting Visigothic expansion northwards and in containing Saxon settlement in the east. Frankish forces were an important component of Aegidius's military strength, fighting for him as either allies, mercenaries or *bucellarii* (some may even have previously been *comitatenses*). Some scholars suggest that the forces of Syagrius and Clovis in 486 would have been even closer in character, since both were reasonably well matched in the numbers and quality of their fighting men. Others have suggested a strong Roman influence on the Merovingian army as a result of Clovis's conquest of Syagrius' kingdom and 'acquisition of his army'. No doubt descendants of Imperial military forces served in Frankish armies (and durable and prestigious items of Roman military equipment could have survived for a couple of generations). Some survivors of Syagrius's army may have transferred their allegiance to Clovis, but we do not know if the latter inherited a functioning Roman organization, nor if the units in later Merovingian armies called *laeti*

C

GAUL, 6th–8th CENTURY

(1) Gallo-Roman aristocratic *miles* from Clermont, c.AD 507

The Gallo-Roman aristocracy of the Auvergne fought alongside the Visigoths against the Franks in the costly defeat at Vouillé in 507. This horseman is represented wearing a magnificent *Spangenhelm* of Eastern Roman origin recovered from the river Saone. His short lamellar armour is an import from Byzantium, copied from a specimen found in Slovenia. The clothing is based on uniquely preserved examples from Roman Egypt, following the colours of the *Vergilius Romanus* miniatures, and note the leather gloves from Trossingen. His main weapons are a 'winged' iron *hasta* from the Capucin graveyard at Bourges, and a *spatha* from the Krefeld Gellep grave. According to Gregory of Tours (IV, 13), the Gallo-Romans used spurs (*calcanei*).

(2) *Miles* of a *Legio Britannica*; Orléans, 530–560

In c.540, St Dalmatius mentioned a 'Breton legion' (*legio Bretonum*) serving at Orléans. Conversely, some scholars identify this with a detachment from the *Secunda Britannica* operating in Gaul, of which we have reconstructed the shield *deigmaton* of a red 8-spoked 'wheel' as illustrated in the *Notitia Dignitatum*. The soldier's general appearance accords with the ivory buckle of the 'Caesarius belt' from Arles, and the *Vergilius Romanus* miniatures. Archaeological elements are copied from the necropolis of Saint-Marcel in Brittany, and the sword is of Chassemy-Pfullingen type, on which Christian ornamentation suggests its use by Gallo-Roman soldiers.

(3) 'Romanus' infantryman, 775–800

Many troops raised by the southern Gallic cities retained military traditions of the Late Roman era, and were described as 'Romani'. Conical *Bandenhelm*-type helmets were often worn over felt or leather hoods. This man wears a *brogne* armour, made of a quilted jacket to which metal and horn scales have been applied. Often a padded corselet alone was used as body protection. The heavy, patterned cloak is of Late Roman origin, and the shield boss with a 'button' apex is of Merovingian style.

Sub-Roman Breton iron 'winged' spearhead and two foliate spearheads, 5th–8th century, from Vieux-Vy-sur-Couesnon. (Musée de Bretagne, inv 976.0067.1–2–3; photos Alain Amet, *licence d'utilisation* CC)

and *milites* in written sources were directly descended from those of the 5th century.

Some of the greatest 5th-century senatorial aristocrats, such as Germanus of Auxerre and Gregory of Tours, had been excluded from the centre of Imperial power, but retained the wealth and private military forces to dominate significant regions. Clovis and his successors manipulated relationships with such leaders to facilitate the rise of the Merovingians.

Armorica and Brittany

Armorica was, according the *Notitia Dignitatum*, under the orders of a single *dux* commanding the local militia and fleet. The frontier command of *Dux tractus Armoricani* was held at different times by important personalities. These included Germanus of Auxerre, and also, in 416, Exuperantius, a *praefectus praetorio Galliarum* who was killed at Arelate in 424, and recorded in *De Reditu Suo* by Claudius Rutilius Namatianus. From the 5th century the Armorican army was recruited on a local basis, sometimes by militarisation of ancient confraternities, such as the *Milites Garronenses* of Blaye; by recently-created units, such as the *Cohors Prima Armorica* at Grannona; or by old units long established in the Roman *provincia*. The local character of these troops, and their subordination to a single authority, help to explain Brittany's gradual acquisition of independence; under local *reges*, it retained the five divisions that had originally formed the basis of the Roman administration. In the 6th century its military leaders retained the title *Comites Brittanorum* (HF, IV, 4). War-bands were composed of both horsemen (probably only the wealthiest) and infantry spearmen.

Post-Roman enclaves and cities

After the conquest of the Auvergne a Gallo-Roman *militia* called *latini* (HF, VIII, 1), under their own *comites*, fought for the Germanic kings (HF, IV, 30). Under Euric, Namatius was a Gallo-Roman 'admiral' who beat off piratical attacks on the Atlantic seaboard. One of the best generals serving the 6th-century king Guntram of the Burgundian Franks was the Gallo-Roman *Patricius* and *Praefectus* Mummolus. The garrisons of cities were under the command of *tribuni* (HF, VII, 24). For larger campaigns Clovis received support from surviving military elements including the private forces of Gallo-Roman magnates, and still-existing units from the Roman army.

In Aquitaine, where Roman institutions remained influential, the garrisons stationed in many walled cities and *castra* were often composed of descendants of Roman soldiers, still commanded by *tribuni* and called *milites* in the 7th century. The mixed ethnicity of the Aquitanian military is illustrated by its incorporation of *Romani*, *Wascones (Vaceti)*, *Aquitani* and *Franci* into various units. Local levies included the *Romani* of Orléans, who opposed Pepin's advance in 761. After the submission of Aquitaine to the Franks, Pepin continued to employ there non-Frankish garrisons of *custodes*, and recognized the legal identity of the *Romani* who formed the main local levies. Under Charlemagne various classes and groups – *Romani* and *laeti*, as well as *Franci* – were established in *centenae*, each commanded by a *centenarius*.

POST-ROMAN BRITAIN

Historical background:
The warlords

According to Gildas, the destruction of Britain as a civilised and Christian community was foreshadowed when the usurper Magnus Maximus (r. 383–388) took troops from the island to fight on the continent (Orosius, VII, 9). These withdrawals, and those of the later usurper Flavius Claudius Constantinus ('Constantine III', r. 407–411), left Britannia without an effective army from 410, and open to attacks by the Picts from the north and the 'Scots' (*Scotti* – then, the term for the Irish) from the west. According to Zosimus, an appeal by loyal British leaders for help from the Emperor Honorius (r.395–423) was rebuffed in the so-called 'Honorian rescript'.

After the Roman field troops' departure, evidence suggests that Britain fragmented into separate political entities largely based on the old regional tribes, at first preserving where possible increasingly shadowy Roman political and administrative structures. Local Celtic military powers were consolidated; leaders are described as surrounded by their military households, and indulging in raids against the lands of rivals. Gildas dismisses these leaders as 'tyrants' who plundered and waged unjust civil wars, and rewarded thieves as their companions: 'They... exalt to the stars... their military companions, bloody, proud and murderous men, adulterers and enemies of God'. He cites as an example the greatest *dux*, Maelgwn Gwynedd; the emergence of these *duces* as military leaders soon led to their description as *reges*, 'kings'. Amid these civil wars and barbarian raids, in 429 the important Gallo-Roman leader Germanus, Bishop of Auxerre, arrived in Britain to combat the Pelagian heresy. According to his *Vita*, Germanus also held the post of *dux*, which explains his military leadership in Britain at the 'battle of the Alleluia'.

In 447/449 a chronic shortage of British manpower during repeated barbarian incursions, against a background of plague, persuaded the south-eastern 'proud tyrant' Vortigern to allow more Saxons to settle in the country in return for military service. Nennius states that he ceded first the Isle of Thanet and subsequently the whole of Kent to two Jutish exiles, the brothers Hengist and Horsa, supplying them with clothing and provisions. (Although this is presented as a turning-point, it was a typical Late Roman solution to a widespread problem. J.N.L. Myres argues from archaeological evidence that Saxon mercenaries had already established communities, particularly in eastern Britain, since the 3rd century.)

The number of Saxons steadily increased, as did their demands, and violent conflicts with the Romano-Britons exploded. The Saxons were usually victorious, storming and burning *civitates* (towns) and massacring their inhabitants as they fought their way into most parts of eastern, midland and northern Britain. Many surviving British communities escaped by crossing the Channel to

The 'Spong man' from Norfolk, 5th century. This pottery lid from a cremation urn, in the shape of a seated male figure measuring 14cm (5½ ins) high, was unearthed in 1979 in the Spong Hill cemetery, and is the earliest Anglo-Saxon three-dimensional human figure ever found. Interestingly, the warrior seems to wear the 'pillbox'-shaped *pileus Pannonicus* cap, as used in the Late Roman army. (Norwich Castle Museum & Art Gallery; photo Wikimedia Commons)

'Minerva and Mars' details from folios 234–235v in the 5th–6th century *Vergilius Romanus* codex. Note the red-crested gilded helmets, the flame-red robes, the god's scale armour, and the large foliate spearhead recalling archaeological finds in Britain. (facsimile; photos Raffaele D'Amato)

Brittany (see above – these included Gildas himself), while others retreated westward and northward into more defensible forested and mountainous terrain (thus their subsequent description as 'Welsh'). An archaeologically confirmed phenomenon of the sub-Roman period in western Britain was the refortification of hillforts, such as South Cadbury in Somerset, and Irthlingborough near Northampton.

Not all Saxons fought against the Romano-Britons, and some were probably found in the ranks of British forces until at least 490. Equally, the Saxon campaigns were not always successful: Vortigern's son Vortimer is recorded as winning a number of victories in the early 450s, and Horsa was killed in batttle at 'Aegelesthrep' (probably Aylesford, Kent). However, it is reported that in *c*.460 Hengist invited Vortigern and many of his noblemen to a banquet to discuss terms, where most were treacherously murdered. The captured Vortigern was then obliged to make major territorial concessions.

Ambrosius

According to Gildas, a conspicuous resistance was finally mounted by a descendant of an aristocratic Roman family, the Aureliani. This Ambrosius Aurelianus was supposedly the son of a Roman officer and a British mother, both slain during the Saxon advance. The 'citizens', as Ambrosius's followers are called, sallied from their refuges and challenged the Saxons in a war which had alternating outcomes. At least one source also suggests a struggle between Ambrosius and Vortigern, and the latter may even have died in a civil war; Gildas describes extensive conflicts among British political entities persisting at the beginning of the 6th century (DEB, 27–32). According to Nennius (48), Ambrosius received the title of *Magnus Rex inter Reges Britanniae* ('Great King among the Kings of Britain'). This might seem to indicate an attempt to unify under a single ruler the Britons and the nominally Roman troops left in Britain, such as the *Equites Taifali* in Lincolnshire. Ambrosius probably united resistance in the west, and ruled directly over the surviving portions of purely Romano-British territory from the Channel right up to Hadrian's Wall. In Welsh he is named Emrys Wledig.

Arthur

While the debate over his existence, identity and status will probably be endless, a general consensus has concluded that, after Ambrosius, a leader named Artorius or 'Arthur' fought against the Saxons in the first part of the 6th century. 'With all the kings and military force of Britain' (*militibus Britanniae*), he won no fewer than 12 battles (HB 50). Modern studies suggest that he was a Romano-Celtic warlord, probably bearing the title *Dux Bellorum* ('war-leader'), who led armoured cavalry against the invading Saxons; Collingwood compares him to a Late Roman cavalry commander. According to Gildas, his masterpiece was the battle of Badon Hill, the 12th victory claimed for him by Nennius, and the culmination of a Romano-

British counter-offensive against the Saxons that had originated under Ambrosius. Gildas describes the battle as *obsessio Badonici montis*, i.e. as the siege of a hill, and as a decisive Romano-British victory, followed by a pause lasting for perhaps half a century in the Anglo-Saxon penetration westwards. Other scholars associate this pause, which is supported by archaeology, with extreme global weather events leading to famine and disease. Notwithstanding attempts to contest the historicity of these British victories (on grounds of their being narrated by later 9th- and 10th-century sources such as the HB and AC), the territories still under control of the Britons retained a significant political, economic and military momentum well into the 6th century. (The criticism that the sources were only written down centuries later is, after all, applicable to about half the history of the human race.)

Gildas does not mention Arthur, but he does name a number of contemporary 'tyrants' (DEB, 27). Gildas probably lived in the time of a certain Dutigirn (mentioned by Nennius – HB, 62, MS3859 BL, folio 188v), who is identified by some scholars as Cyndeyrn ap Cyngar. Both Arthur and the leading warrior Urien ap Rheged appear in the *Harleian Genealogies*, a collection of Old Welsh genealogies preserved in the BM Harley manuscript dated 1100, but compiled from oral traditions during the life of Owain ap Hywel Ida (*c*.988). The famous bard Taliesin was a contemporary of Arthur and Urien, and wrote praise-poetry about both, in *The Chair of the Sovereign* and *Urien of Yrechwydd*. The *Annales Cambriae*, presumed to have been transcribed in the mid-10th century, narrate further deeds by and the death of Arthur – another proof of the existence of at least an oral tradition claiming him as an historical character. According to the AC, after a series of victorious campaigns both on the continent and in Britain, Arthur was involved in a civil war against his nephew Mordreaut (Mordred), and died after the battle of Camlann in 537 or 543 (AC, CW. 125.6–126.3).

Kingdoms

After Arthur, the divided petty kingdoms were unable to stop either the interrupted but progressive Germanic expansion or the incursions of Picts and Irish, but fierce local resistance allowed the Romano-Britons ('Welsh') to survive in some strongholds derived from Roman *civitates* (towns) or based on refurbished Celtic hillforts. During the 6th–8th centuries the transition from Romano-British *civitates* to Welsh kingdoms must have been bloody and confused. The Saxon triumphs at Deorham (577, probably in south Gloucestershire), and at Chester (604/616?) helped divide the surviving centres of resistance, severing the land connections between modern Devon and Cornwall, Wales, and the kingdoms in the north and Scotland.

Bryneichn Formed from the southern lands of the Votadini, possibly as part of the division of the militarised Roman 'Old North' (*Yr Hen Ogledd*) after Coel Hen's death in 420 (see below). The kingdom may have been ruled from Din Guardi (Bamburgh), falling to the Saxons in 604.

Detail from graffiti representing fighting warriors, 6th–8th century, on a slate from Tintagel Castle, Cornwall. (Drawing by Andrea Salimbeti, ex Thorpe, 1988)

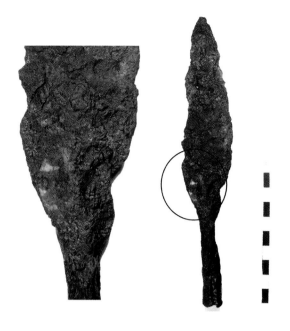

Two images of a spearhead found with the warrior burial under the Lowbury Hill barrow in Berkshire. The burial is dated to c.650–700, and, despite its location, analysis of the warrior's teeth strongly suggests that he was a native of western Cornwall in the ancient Dumnonian kingdom. Only after conservation was it recognized that the spearhead originally bore (circled) a round enamel inlay decoration in green, red and yellow on both sides of the blade, making it a unique specimen without parallel in England. Enamelling is considered to be a Romano-Celtic rather than a Germanic technique, and where it occurs in Anglo-Saxon contexts it is usually taken to indicate the presence of Celtic craftsmen. This leaf-shaped spearhead has an overall length of 196mm (7¾ ins) and is 37mm (1½ ins) wide at its broadest. (Photos courtesy of Oxfordshire Museum)

Reghed and Cumbria During the Late Roman occupation proxy local rulers or *Duces Brittanniarum* had governed the northern region. The last of these was Coel Hen ('Old King Cole' of the nursery rhyme), who lived c.350–420; his kingdom covered the area from north of modern Liverpool up to Hadrian's Wall, and stretched from coast to coast. It was later divided into smaller polities between his descendants. According to the rudimentary sources, upon the death of Coel Hen's son, Mor ap Ceneu, northern Britain was divided into Ebrauc to the east of the Pennines and Rheged to the west, and in 535 the latter was separated into North Rheged and South Rheged. Rheged or Cumbria emerged as the region's most powerful kingdom under Urien (c.530–590), a descendant of Coel Hen. He ruled from Carlisle at the western end of Hadrian's Wall, which retained a Romanised ruling elite and institutions. While the patchwork of kindoms east of the Pennines increasingly fell to the Bernician Anglo-Saxons, Rheged remained a bulwark of Romano-British defence until its fall in 730.

Elmet (or Elfed) also apparently emerged during the late 5th-century fragmentation of Coel Hen's kingdom. It occupied the territory between the river Humber and Hadrian's Wall, with some extensions north of the latter, and seems to have been a quasi-continuation of the Roman military zone in the north. Once it fell to the Saxons in 617, any realistic British hope of holding onto the Pennines disappeared.

Gododdin Archaeology suggests that a local Romano-Christian elite held control in a region spanning modern north-east England and south-east Scotland until its extinction in the mid-7th century. Here the tribal Votadini and their successors, the Manaw Gododdin, formed a kingdom which is immortalised by the eponymous late 6th-century poem. *Y Gododdin* is a commemorative lament for the heroes gathered by the lord of Din Eidyn (modern Edinburgh) to do battle with the Saxon invaders of Deira at Catraeth (Catterick, Yorkshire). Although the region had only occasionally formed part of the Empire, the poem bears witness to the warriors' fellow-feeling with other Romano-Britons. Gododdin fell to the Saxons of Bernicia in c.640.

Strathclyde South-west and western-central Scotland was perhaps historically inhabited by a people called the Damnoni/Damnonii, though they are only mentioned in one 2nd-century source. The first reference to a possible mid-5th-century kingdom ruled by a king Ceretic (Coroticus/Guletic) is a letter from St Patrick. The dynasty was probably well established by the end of the 6th century, extending from at least the Firth of Clyde south-westwards down into Cumbria. Its rulers were *reges* of Alo Cluathe/Alt Clut ('Kings of the Clyde Rock'; HEi,1), with a formidable fortress at Dùn Breatann ('Fort of the Britons'). Annexed by the Northumbrian Saxons at the beginning of the 7th century, Strathclyde was liberated in 685 after the battle of Nechtanesmere. In c.750 Strathclyde was threatened by an alliance between Northumbrians and Picts, and the Northumbrians wrested much of the western territory from the Britons, forcing them into submission in 756.

Gwynned, Dyfed and Powys

Fortified sites from the 5th–7th centuries have been interpreted as power-centres associated with an emergent post-Roman elite, with residences localised at Dinas Emrys in north-west Wales and Bwrdd Arthur on Anglesey ('Ambrosius's Town' and 'Arthur's Table', respectively.) At the end of the 6th century the tribal territory of the ancient Ordovices in north Wales gave birth to Gwynned, probably militarily the strongest of the kingdoms in *Britannia Prima*. Gildas also writes of Vortiporius, 'tyrant of the Demetae', based on the *civitas* which would become the kingdom of Dyfed in the south-west, where a Romano-British elite remained identifiable until as late as the 11th century.

According to Kenneth Dark, the *civitas* of the ancient Silures split in the 6th century into Gwent in eastern Wales (derived from Roman Caerwent – Venta Silurum), and Glywysing (Glamorgan) to its west, ruled by hillfort-dwelling chieftains. The *Llandaff Charters* indicate that during the 5th–8th centuries other major and minor kingdoms existed, including Ceredigion, Builth, and Gower. The 7th–8th centuries brought consolidations, with the seats of the high kings of Wales variously in Glamorgan in the north-west, Deheubarth in the south, and Powys in eastern central Wales. Smaller entities were absorbed, and their kings reduced in status to leading men or *uchelwyr*.

Dinas Powys was the most important centre in Wales in the 5th–7th centuries. It housed the court of a chieftain among a Romano-Celtic aristocracy, who attracted warriors around them in mimicry of Imperial government. The poetic work ascribed to Taliesin, in praise of Selyf's father Cynan, suggests that this king of Powys launched an aggressive series of successful campaigns against other Welsh leaders, including an expedition right across Gwynedd into Anglesey. In the successive centuries Powys would form a formidable alliance with neighbouring Mercia against Saxon Northumbria.

Dumnonia

The *civitas* of the Dumnonii, who inhabited Cornwall and Devon, would become the kingdom of Dyfneint. Late 5th-century Dumnonia gives the impression of being one of the most thriving parts of Britain, probably capable of fielding a reasonably strong military force. With its long coastlines and maritime tradition, it was well placed to transport troops both across the Channel and also around Brittany. According to Gildas, it was ruled by the 'tyrant' Constantine (Custennin, son of Cynfawr, son of Duke Cador of Cornwall). Archaeology reveals the minting in pewter of possible royal coins or tokens with the image of a *rex* – perhaps Elabius, who was met by Germanus of Auxerre in 429. Kenneth Dark hypothesizes that the elites of 5th–6th century Dumnonia, derived at least in part from those of the Romano-British *civitas*, ruled sub-kingdoms based on hillforts, all owing allegiance to the ruler of the whole of Dumnonia based at Tintagel.

Other Romano-British enclaves

At Lowbury Hill, just off the Ridgeway at Aston Upthorpe, Berkshire, a rich warrior burial of *c.*650–700 has been unearthed close to an old Roman temple site overlooking Wallingford ('Welsh people's ford'), which was a native, rather than a Saxon settlement. A unique enamel decoration on his spearhead

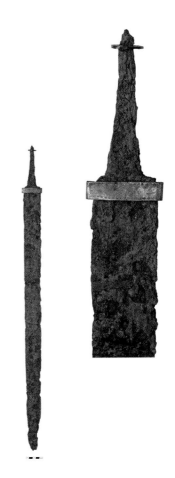

Two images of the Lowbury Hill warrior's scabbarded sword, which was found lying with its hilt on his breast. Analysis suggests that its high-quality pattern-welded blade was older than its owner, who died at over 50 years of age. This supports the obviously convincing hypothesis that high-quality swords might pass down from generation to generation. (Photos courtesy of Oxfordshire Museum)

is interpreted as of Celtic workmanship. Isotope analysis of the teeth shows a strong likelihood that the Lowbury warrior was a Celtic Briton who grew up in west Cornwall, thus suggesting that post-Roman Britons retained a significant presence in the Berkshire area later than previously thought.

Similarly, through analysis of patterns of cemetery sites, Dark has attempted to demonstrate that, at least in the 6th century, eastern Britain was a patchwork of communities rather than a homogenous Anglo-Saxon zone. Some were wholly British or of mixed origin, and Romano-British enclaves (like Deira in the north) did survive for some time.

MILITARY ORGANIZATION

Warlord armies

The military command of Upper (*Prima*, southern) and Lower (*Secunda*, northern) Britain in the early 5th century was held by three generals: the *Comes Britanniae*; the *Comes Litoris Saxonici* ('Count of the Saxon Shore', in south-east Britain); and the *Dux Britanniarum*. References by Gildas and Nennius suggest that the *Comes Britanniae* ('Count of Britain') commanded a mobile, mainly cavalry field army. The *Dux Britanniarum* ('Duke' or 'Leader of the Britons') defended the northern frontier, being responsible, according to the *Notitia Dignitatum*, for the Hadrian's Wall forts. By the 5th century the *Dux Britanniarum's* frontier troops stationed in the Wall region were often hereditary – i.e., sons followed fathers into units that thus became wholly localised.

This last general's title is tantalisingly similar to *Dux Bellorum* ('War-Leader'), given by Nennius to Arthur; but there is no reason to think that this is a misremembered Roman title. Comparable Welsh titles were *Llywiaudir llawur* ('Battle-Ruler') and *Tywyssawc Cat*. Gildas calls Ambrosius a *dux* perhaps simply as the heir to the last Imperially-appointed Roman army authority in Britain, and *Dux Bellorum* was probably applied in this generic sense to other figures such as Arthur.

Part of the rationale for the 7th-century Saxon settlement of the north – to fight off the Scottish Picts and the Irish *Scotti* – was presumably the absence of any other surviving garrisons in the Wall zone. However, according to the analysis by Dark, some Wall forts had been reoccupied and refortified during the 6th-century 'Badon generation'. A 6th-century inscription at Vindolanda names a local Romano-British warlord as Brigomaglus, perhaps co-ruling with a certain Riacus. An invigorated British resistance in *Britannia Secunda* might even have seen the population appoint their own *dux*. In using this title of Arthur, Nennius may actually be making a point about the different nature of his military authority as *dux* from the civil, taxing and quasi-judicial role of the *reges* ('kings'). In this case Arthur or other warlords would be fighting as *duces bellorum* under the actual rule of mutually co-operating kings of the Britons.

Any 'Arthurian task force' of armoured riders, logically modelled on Late Roman cavalry, would be characterized by speedy mobility. At that time it was quite common for such contingents to be called upon to

The *umbo* of the Lowbury Hill warrior's shield, which had apparently been laid across his knees; compare with that in the 'Turnus and Iris' miniature on page 11. He had also been buried with a knife in his hand. A beautiful hanging bowl was found tilted against the side of the grave, above a comb in a leather case. A buckle, a bone cloak-fastener and traces of his woven clothing were still recognizable. (Photo courtesy of Oxfordshire Museum)

Detail from tomb of 'St Constantine', believed to have been a martyred 6th-century missionary to the Picts. The carving seems to represent a mounted king of Strathclyde; note the beard, the bladed weapon at his left hip, and the suggestion of either a falling crest or long hair. 9th century, *in situ* Govan Old Parish Church Museum. (Photo Tom Horne, courtesy of Govan Heritage Trust).

help a small, threatened kingdom, and if necessary a cavalry unit might have travelled about 40 miles per day. In the 5th–6th centuries the comprehensive network of Roman roads would still have been in relatively good condition. Additionally, Britannia had been for centuries an importer of equine bloodstock, such as Frisian horses; this, and a strong Celtic cavalry tradition, also favour the theory of a mobile cavalry capable of campaigning over large areas of Britain.

Nennius calls soldiers of all origins *milites*, who fought for booty or for reward from their *duces*, but uses the term *exercitus* (army) only for anti-Saxon forces. The only formation mentioned is the generic 'battle-line'. We have no indication of the size of a 'typical' Romano-British army of the warlord period. The *duces* may be imagined as bringing their military followings to combine into larger armies under the greater rulers. As in Gaul, there were presumably diverse systems. In the militarised north, and possibly in south-east Wales, leaders of old army families might have employed surviving elements of the Roman military as their war-band, while in west and north Wales the leaders of ancient territorial entities would have had their own military 'family' or *teulu*.

From the analyses by Alcock, British warfare in this period seems to have been an open-field affair characterized by mobility, with concentrations for clashes on major highways and at river crossings, where defenders would try to intercept fast-moving raiders. Some scholars believe that memories survived of the disciplined battle formations and tactics of the legions. While Gildas condemned the Britons of the immediate post-Roman period for fighting their enemies with 'no orderly square, no right wing or other apparatus of war', this complaint indicates that such tactics were at least still known in his day, and were expected of competent commanders.

Romano-British kingdoms

Royal dynasties emerged within Wales by at least the late 5th century. Durotrigian hillforts probably represented royal centres south of the Wansdyke, where there is a relative lack of evidence for surviving urban centres. Urban elite residences in Romano-British towns survived north of the Wansdyke, where a bureaucracy-based society survived until the 7th century. Both areas preserved features of Late Roman Christian society, and many inscriptions in Wales and in south-west England alike confirm the extent of the Latin language and titles among British elites. Geoffrey of Monmouth gives the Romano-British general Brocmail the style 'consul of the city' at the battle of Chester in 616. However, in a praise-poem following his victory over the Saxons only a few years later in the 630s, Cadwallon of Gwynedd is simply called 'lord of' or 'leader' of the hosts of' Britain. In the north, *Y Gododdin* focuses on heroic deeds in battle, and the bonds of loyalty cemented through celebrations in the mead hall. Nevertheless, one Tutvwlch is specifically given the title *rector* (YG B8) and the epithet 'helmsman', and forces are led by a 'regulator of hosts' or 'one who marshalled the armies'.

Archaeological evidence from defended centres such as Dinas Powys and Dinas Emrys shows that royal households were able to accumulate considerable wealth. The research of G.R.J. Jones paints a picture of post-Roman Welsh society dominated by aristocratic military elites, supported by the labour of bondmen working the land. A number of Welsh townships (*trefi*; sing. *tref*) were inhabited by either free or bond tenants, holding land in return for providing food rents and military and labour services. The small size of Romano-British forts of the late 5th and 6th centuries is directly related to the contemporary military organization. In post-Roman Wales and Cornwall, as in much of contemporary continental Europe, military obligation was personal and individual rather than in complete territorial groups.

Little is known of the organization of the Church in early medieval Wales, but there are suggestions that senior churchmen behaved little differently from secular rulers, and would lead their own forces to battle. Later bards celebrated St Tysilio, a son of Brocmail Ysgithrog, as a warrior saint who fought at the battle of Maserfelth in 643. In the *Life of St Cadog*, a late 11th-century work purporting to tell a 6th-century tale, the saint is portrayed as a lord dominating his country, surrounded by a household force (*familia*) including 100 horsemen (*milites*) and associated with a fort (*oppidum*).

D **'BATTLE OF THE ALLELUIA'; BRITAIN, AD 429**

(1) Bishop Germanus of Auxerre, *Dux Proelli*

The *Life of St Germanus* (III, 16–17) recounts that this aristocratic Gallo-Roman churchman and soldier (at one time appointed the *Dux tractus Armoricani*) organized a Romano-British army to oppose Pictish and Saxon raiders. On the day of battle he led his whole army in giving a great shout of 'Alleluia!', which supposedly startled their attackers into retreating before combat could be joined. Germanus is described in his *Life* (I, 4) as always wearing a short *cucullus* (here with the hood thrown back) over a *tunica*. We have given him a ringmail *lorica* based on fragments from Humshaugh, Northumberland (PAS NCL-673E41), Gallo-Roman weapons from finds at Pouan, the Alfriston belt from East Sussex and the Faversham brooch from Kent.

(2) Romano-British *miles*, ex *Legionis Sextae Britanniorum*

The last reference to what had been the old Legio VI Victrix is found in the *Notitia Dignitatum*, which lists it under the *Dux Britanniorum*. A rectangular belt-buckle found at Traprain Law,

East Lothian, was typical of troops in the Illyrian diocese, suggesting that the owner was a Gothic soldier in the Roman army, recruited and armed in the Danubian area; this was supported by the find of a woman's brooch in the same hoard, perhaps belonging to the soldier's wife. We have given him the Burgh Castle helmet from Norfolk, while his Coptic-style garments and the blazon on his shield are from the recently-found mosaic at Boxford, Berkshire, and his Romano-Germanic style of *spatha* is from Blacknall Field, Pewsey, Wiltshire.

(3) Romano-British leader

This reconstruction is based on a statuette of an early 5th-century cavalryman, and the *Vergilius Romanus* miniatures. Note his iron and copper-alloy *squama*, and the set of javelins carried in a quiver on the off-side of the horse. We take his dagger from the splendid example found at Richborough, Kent, with a facetted silver-gilt pommel and scabbard-mounts. The sword is based on that from Brighthampton, Oxfordshire; its scabbard chape is decorated in 'quoit-brooch' style, and it also bears a small silver cross patée.

a

b

(a) 5th–7th century javelin head, from Four Crosses, Llandysilio, Powys. Unearthed in a ditch near some possibly early-medieval burials, this and another find were attributed by Leslie Alcock to Cadwallon's 7th-century army from Gwynned. It measures 74cm (29 ins) overall, with a relatively short leaf-shaped blade on a long, slender iron shank with an integral socket, recalling that of a Roman legionary *pilum*. (Photo courtesy of National Museum of Wales)

(b) 5th–6th century Romano-British spearhead from the Thames, London. It is 55.5cm (21¾ ins) long, with a thin closed socket 18mm (⅔ in) in diameter, secured to the shaft by two rivets. It once had 'wings', which have corroded away, and has a strong midrib. While reminiscent of some late La Tène examples, it has no known exact parallels, so could be specific to the Romano-Britons. (Private British collection; photo courtesy of Dan Shadrake).

Teulu, Gosgordd and *Nifer*

The earliest leaders of post-Roman Britain rose to prominence as commanders of personal war-bands raised in their own localities; this armed force was their *comitatus* (in Latin), or *teulu* ('family', in Welsh; plur. *teuluoedd*). The *Y Gododdin* hosting, *teulu Dewr*, was 'the war-band [of or for] Deira', its objective. The brothers of Gwion ap Cyndrwyn, one of the leaders killed at the 7th-century battle of Chester, were said in the poems of Cynddylan to command as *penteulu*, suggesting the leader of a sizeable troop. (However, Roman titles also survived in tales of Welsh saints: St Cybi's father was *princeps militia* for a king in Cornwall, and the military term *dux cohortis* was used to describe St Padarn's leadership of a band of monks.)

While the *penteulu* might lead (part of?) his lord's forces into battle while his master remained at court, military leadership was still an essential part of kingship. In *Y Gododdin*, the king Mynyddog Mwynfawr was responsible for gathering the force sent to Catraeth, but took no personal part in the expedition. For reasons of pride, members of a war-band sometimes resented being subordinated to anyone but their king. They also objected to sharing the glory and loot with even well-born foreign hostages attached to the court, or with paid mercenaries.

Gosgordd is usually translated as 'retinue', but has been suggested as representing a force larger than the *teulu*, though its inclusion of domestic elements makes it more difficult to interpret in a purely military context. *Y Gododdin* always refers to the *gosgordd*, rather than the *teulu*, of Mynyddog Mwynfawr (YG, XI, XXXI). In that poem the former term may mean only the leadership element, and the latter a subdivision of a larger force. A variety of terms is used for 'host' or 'army' and these should be differentiated from the *gosgordd*. In later sources, such as the *Triads*, there is little to choose between the 'Three Faithful War-bands [*teulu*]' of Britain and the 'Three Noble Retinues [*gosgordd*]'; both refer to forces that fought at Arderydd in 573, and each is said to have comprised 2,100 men.

The other term regularly associated with *teulu* is *nifer*, though it is rarely found in early texts. *Nifer*, which in modern Welsh is translated as 'number', might be compared to the Latin *numerus*, a generic term for any military unit. However, in the 9th-century *Canu Heledd* poem cycle, purporting to tell a 7th-century story, references suggest the meaning of an entire courtly household rather than the militarised *teulu*.

Sometimes the sources describe a lord's military followers as his *milites*, *satellites* (bodyguards), or *tirones* (recruits).

Size of armies

For the war-band of a petty prince, the figure of between 50 and 100 might be reasonable, and for such a small force the modest size of the known fortifications would be appropriate. The *teulu* formed the core of a Welsh leader's military power, and when a greater host was required this core played a key role in gathering and leading it. Presumably, each member of the *teulu* might be responsible for assembling a certain number of troops. Such armies might have the character of a national levy intended to represent 'all the Britons': the *Triads* speak of Arthur assembling the army (*llu*) of the 'Island of Britain', and in the *Mabinogion* Brân musters 'all of Britain' for his expedition to Ireland, gathering 'the full complement of districts [*gwledydd*]' and leaving only seven leaders to defend the homeland.

The sources suggest the presence on campaign of rustic levied infantry as well as the mounted elite; for instance, in Taliesin's poems *pedyt* (from the Latin *pedites*) are described cheering Urien's return from a successful raid. However, it is very difficult to estimate the size of such field forces. There are few unambiguous references to numbers, which must have varied greatly according to the power, needs and personality of a lord, and the size and geography of his territory. *Pa gur*, a fragmentary Old Welsh poem from the *Black Book of Carmarthen* transcribed perhaps *c.*1100, gives figures of 600 and 900 men for the size of a Romano-British army.

For the exceptional enterprise narrated in *Y Gododdin* – the British attempt to overthrow the nascent Anglo-Saxon kingdom of Deira – 300 warriors were mustered, supposedly from several kingdoms but principally from south-east Scotland. The poem actually gives a figure of 363 (YG XXI: 'Three heroes and three score and three hundred, [the former?] wearing the golden torques'). However, these were only the commanding elite of the *gosgordd* (*Tri si chatvarchawc*), covered with gold and armoured (*Eidyn euruchawc, Tri llu llurugawc*), under three leaders wearing golden torques (*Tri eur deyrn dorchawc*). These mounted and armoured 'officers' might each have been accompanied by a body of levied foot-soldiers, giving a total army of up to 2,000–3,000 men. The language of the passage is unclear, saying both that each unit was formed of 100 men (YG XVIII : *Pymwnt a phymcant*, 'five battalions of 100 men each'), and that each 'head' (*cwn*) commanded 300 men (*Trychwn a thrychant*, 'three levies of 300 each'). According to Alcock, such a mixed cavalry and infantry force could have covered the 130 miles between Dere Street and the Tees valley north of Catterick in ten days.

At Chester in 616, Selyf of Powys is likely to have brought a significant military host to the battle; he summoned the *reguli* of his realm, who would each have brought their own household forces. Writing of the 630s, Bede was horrified by the presence in Northumbria of Cadwallon of Gwynedd 'and his vast forces *(copiis)*, which he boasted were irresistible'. At the battle of Winwaed in 654, the HB says that the force led by Cynddylan was composed of 700 'lords', several of whom are named. These aristocratic war-bands may be seen as a full-time professional military elite, while the free peasantry were a part-time but none the less semi-regular army; in battle they stood arranged according to their several banners. The military system was supported by the entire productive capacity of the land.

EQUIPMENT, ARMS & CLOTHING

For the 5th and early 6th centuries one of the most important iconographic sources for Britain and Gaul may be the *Vergilius Romanus* codex (Cod.Vat. lat. 3867). Dated by Weitzmann to the second half of the 5th century, it is considered by several authorities, including Martin Henig and Kenneth Dark, to be a Romano-British manuscript. If true, it is the earliest such document known, and its miniatures represent an invaluable source for the military and civil material culture of sub-Roman Britain and Brittany.

If iconography from the successive centuries is scarce, the literary references are abundant, and the archaeology gives us some help. While it is undeniable that most goods found in Anglo-Saxon graves belong to their own material culture, we should remember that in the 5th and early 6th centuries many Saxon mercenaries had Roman equipment; that war booty was commonplace; and that there was frequent intermarriage with British women. The archaeological evidence for such mixing of cultures, rather than straightforward replacement, is consistent. It is therefore no surprise to find tools, weapons and costume-fittings of Romano-Celtic origin in Saxon graves – Roman culture had a massive impact on the Germanic peoples. The same would be true in reverse; in succeeding centuries Britons, Armoricans and Gallo-Romans made wide use of Saxon and Frankish weapons and costume elements. These reciprocal influences generated mixed accoutrements of Romano-Germanic splendour.

GALLO-ROMAN *PATRICII* ARMIES

Helmets
Sidonius Appolinaris mentions Gallo-Roman leaders wearing burnished helmets (*cassides*) with red, gold or reddish-yellow crests (SA, *Paneg.* VII, 241), as visible in the *Vergilius Romanus* miniatures. The conical crest-base reminds us of period examples of the *Spangenhelm*, like those from Vézeronce or the river Saône. Like those specimens, the helmets worn by

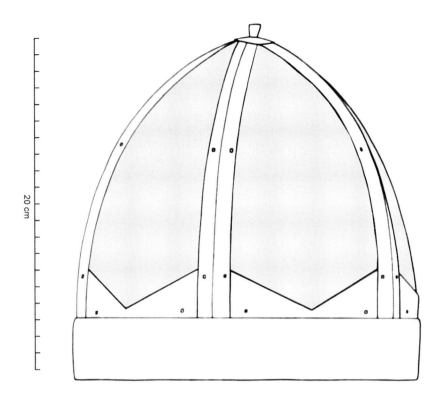

Attempted reconstruction of a 6th–7th century *Spangenhelm* from Allerey-sur-Saône. We cannot exclude the attachment of pendant cheek and/or neck-pieces to such helmets by a means not requiring rivets through the brow-band; see photo on page 4. (Drawing by Andrea Salimbeti, ex-Bailly, 1990)

20 cm

patrician commanders had flexible cheek-pieces (*de concavo tibi cassidis exituro flexilium laminarum vincula:* '[others] undid the flexible cheek-pieces of the helmet [you were eager to] remove').

Body armour

Gallo-Roman patricians seem mainly to have worn either ringmail or scale armour, the latter historically termed *squama* in Latin; however, by the 5th century this might refer to either scale or lamellar armour. The corselet of Ecdicius Avitus, 'clotted with gore', is called a *lorica* (SA, *Pan..* VII, 262), the term applied to iron ringmail, which he wore together with laced greaves (SA, *Ep*. III, 3). *Lorica* is also the term used for the armour of Calminius, defender of Clermont (SA, *Ep*.V, XII).

Both faces of a 5th–6th century sub-Roman Gallic helmet cheek-guard from Lyon. (Museum de Lyon-Fourvière, inv Br 282; photo Raffaele D'Amato, courtesy of the Museum)

Weapons

The weapons of these warlords were the long *contus* cavalry spear and the sword. The combination of helmet and scale or lamellar armour accords with the image of the Late-Roman heavy armoured cavalryman, charging with what we would call a lance (SA, *Pan*.VII, 290–294). Other weapons mentioned are javelins (*jacula*), and the bow (*arcus*), as also used for the hunt (SA, *Ep*. I, 2; III, 2). The 'winged' spear (*venabulum; Ep*. VIII, 6) was used for boar-hunting, but probably

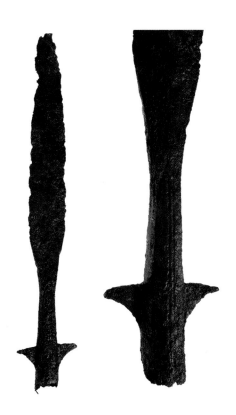

also for war, which explains the number of 5th-century specimens found in Gaul. Swords (*gladii*; SA, *Ep*.VII, 7) are widely mentioned, but archaeology reveals long Romano-Germanic *spathae*. Grave 68 at Charleville-Mézières in the Ardennes, dated by Kazanski to the Merovingian I period between 470 and 530, yielded a sword with a 'quoit-brooch' style guard, bird-head decorations, and a decorated cloisonné buckle plate. Such features are characteristic of elite burials, and this grave, certainly belonging to a Germanic warrior, may exemplify the type of weaponry used by Syagrius's army.

Other equipment

The *signa* (standards) carried were those of the Christian Late Empire, i.e. *vexilla* and *labara*, but also *dracones*. Horses are mentioned with bridles (*pinguia*) and saddles (*sellae*). A possible Gallo-Roman horse-bit, with two lateral rods and adorned with bird-heads, was also found in Grave 68 at Charleville-Mézières. Parallels from Bylym-Kudinetovo suggest that they belong to the Eastern Roman tradition, in which representations of eagles are widespread. Bird-head decorations on e.g. horse-harnesses and sword scabbards are common in northern Gaul from the second half of the 5th century.

Two images of a sub-Roman 7th-century iron 'winged' spearhead from Rennes, Brittany. (Musée de Bretagne, inv 926.0038.3; photos Alain Amet, *licence d'utilisation* CC)

Military dress

Over the long-sleeved tunic, the various cloaks most common in Late Roman times were probably worn, e.g. the *pallium*, of Greek origin, and the Roman *paenula* for travel or bad weather. Sidonius (*Ep.* to Domitius, II, 2) mentions garments of linen (*carbasus*) and silk (*bombyx*), and the use of a thick, rough cloak (*endromis*) to protect against cold and rain. He also mentions *fasciae* (puttee-like wrappings) on the legs.

 BRITISH WARLORD ARMIES

(1) Romano-British *Dux Bellorum (Amerawdwr)*, early 6th century
While this suggested reconstruction of Arthur at the battle of Mount Badon obviously can be no more than imaginary, it is based on early poetic sources as well as some comparable archaeology. The highly decorated helmet, sheathed in silver-gilt and decorated with coloured glass gems, is of 4th-century Budapest typology. The 12th-century writer Layamon, drawing on earlier oral sources, described Arthur's helmet as 'of steel very high, and many gemstones in it, all set in gold'; we have also given it an expensive imported peacock-feather crest. The gilded copper-alloy *lamellar* armour, the gold-decorated tunic and purple *paludamentum* all correspond with Late Roman styles. Layamon mentions his 'legs… covered with hose of steel', which we replace with more plausible splinted armour. The device on his shield, according to the HB, was the cross of Christ, here copied from the shield with the *Chi-rho* monogram carved on one of the 6th-century Kirkmadrine stones from Galloway. We cannot exclude that the image of the Virgin Mary was the personal standard of Arthur. Though hardly visible here, the legendary sword 'Excalibur' (*Caledvwlch*) is copied from Welsh fragments, the hilt decorated according to the Celtic style described in the *Mabinogion*.

(2) Romano-British *pedyt*; Dyfed, late 5th–early 6th century
This simple infantryman is clothed in Celtic style, including a chequered cloak fastened with a bi-metal brooch from Cadbury Camp, and wears a leather *lluric* as his main protection. His spear and dagger are taken from finds at Coygan Camp. The *deigmaton* on his shield is copied from that of the *Defensores Seniores* in the *Notitia Dignitatum*.

(3) Standard-bearer of *loricati*; Rheged, early 6th century
According to legend, Arthur's Cumbrian standard-bearer – the *Gwres ap Rheged* – carried a red *draco*; this reconstruction of its copper-alloy head follows a miniature image on a sub-Roman sword-fitting from Goldcliff, Monmouthshire. We reconstruct the gilded ridge-helmet from fragments found at Greens Norton, Northamptonshire, and give him an iron scale *lluryg*, as mentioned by Aneirin (XV) being worn in his time (second half of the 6th century). Just visible are a precious gold torque of rank around his neck, and an annular brooch from Bath, Somerset, used to fasten his heavy fur-lined woollen winter cloak.

Iron 7th–8th century javelin head from the ancient Abbey of Landévennec, Brittany; excavations by A. Bardel (ex-UMR CNRS 6566) and R. Pérennec (Conseil Départementale du Finistèrre). (Photo courtesy of G. Couix, Ancient Abbey Museum Collection)

The dress (*vestis*) of the Gallo-Roman nobles, like Vectius (SA, *Ep.*, IV, 9), was always splendid, with decorated accoutrements and horse-harness. Even their hairstyle was characteristic: one land-owner had his hair cut 'wheel-fashion' (IV. XIII. I; *crinis in rotae specimen accisus*) – probably a reference to the Late Roman style visible in 5th-century artworks. But there is also evidence of Gallo-Romans dressing as Germans, and copying their behaviour. Sidonius complains about certain men who 'like to march to a banquet bearing arms (*armati*)... attend a funeral in white (*albati*)... go to church in furs (*pelliti*), and hear a litany [dressed in] beaver-pelts (*castorinati*)'.

Hunters or peasants are often represented in the 5th century dressed in loose tunics worn bloused, usually with long sleeves; vents under the armpits allowed the arms to be slipped out of the sleeves, which were then tied behind the neck. Legwear was short breeches or none, with puttees (*fasciae crurales*) or gaiters (*tibiales*), and high shoes of *calcei* type.

Germanic equipment

The descriptions of Frankish rulers allied to the Empire give a picture of wealth and splendour to match the richest Gallo-Roman leaders. The prince Sigismer (SA, *Ep.* IV, 20), when visiting his prospective father-in-law, the Burgundian monarch Chilperic, rides a steed whose harness is decorated with *phalerae*, and the mounts of his escort have flashing gems (*radiantibus gemmis*) on their *antilina* and *postilina*. Sigismer is dressed in a flame-red mantle, with much glint of 'ruddy' gold (*flameus cocco, rutilus auro*), and gleam of 'snowy' silken tunic (*lacteus serico*).

The elements found in the grave in Tournai, Belgium, of Childeric, allied to Syagrius, confirm that this king was armed and equipped like a *magister militum*, with weapons and belts decorated with precious gemstones, and he was even accompanied in death by the severed head of a harnessed warhorse. His seal-ring represents him half-length, wearing a Roman scale corselet. As governor of the province of *Belgica Secunda* he wears a Roman officer's cloak (*paludamentum*), and, like Roman emperors on their coins, holds a spear in his right hand. Unlike them, however, he is depicted bareheaded, with his long hair braided according to Frankish royal custom (HF, II, 9). The mixed culture of Germanic *foederati* defending the Empire is evident in this image. Childeric was buried in his purple *paludamentum* decorated with gold thread, and fixed at the right shoulder with a cruciform *fibula* of Byzantine style.

Childeric's grave-goods also included a massive solid-gold bracelet; several button-like studs, belt- and harness-buckles; shoes with kidney-shaped plates in gold and garnet cloisonné work; and a probable belt-pouch with a garnet clasp. He was also buried with a spear as a symbol of command, and a typical Frankish throwing-axe (*francisca*). Other richly-decorated weapons are early examples of the spread of the polychrome style to Gaul. A long *spatha*, the gold hilt adorned with garnets and a pommel with equine *protomes*, had an equally impressive scabbard. A *scramasax* (a long, single-edged Frankish knife with a plain, narrow handle) was found in a scabbard adorned with wavy cloisonné and a border of cabuchons. Virtually all researchers agree on the Mediterranean origin of this furniture, perhaps the products of a Byzantine or Italian workshop.

As to the warriors led by such resplendent leaders, we read of tight, knee-length tunics of varied colours, with sleeves covering only the upper arms; low boots of 'bristly' hide; and either green cloaks with crimson borders, or, in the Rhineland, of animal-skin. Swords hung from shoulder-baldrics, and warriors carried barbed javelins and *francisca* axes. The wealthier men had shields with 'tawny-golden' bosses and 'snowy-silver' edges.

BRITTANY AND ARMORICA

Here the aristocracy long retained a warrior culture. Once initial conquest and expansion had been achieved, war remained a source of royal prestige, immediate booty, and continuing tribute in livestock and foodstuffs to distribute among the community (HF, IX, 24). Acts of 'social theatre', such as funerals with deposition of rich objects in graves, were important as a means of competitive display. The island of Lavret has yielded graves containing finds associated with Breton horsemen, and, by some scholars, with immigrant aristocrats from Dumnonia, who raised a nearby monastery in about 460. Generally, later funerary finds dated from the 7th century onwards show Merovingian influence.

Helmets

The helmets used by the *Britanni* were certainly of Late Roman typology. Benjamin Franckaert has pointed out the similarity of various helmets in the *Vergilius Romanus* miniatures to the Krivina 1 find from Iatrus, Bulgaria, dated to the mid-5th century, with characteristic cheek-guards and slots for a crest, but lacking a nose-guard (as also represented in the mosaics of Sta Maria Maggiore, *c*.432). Sources for helmets used in Armorica in subsequent centuries are scarce. We may speculate continuing employment of various

'Humility versus Pride', in a 9th-century illustrated manuscript. Various Carolingian manuscripts of the period show, beside the employment of ringmaill and scale, a wide distribution of pseudo-Roman armours. In all probability these reflect the equipment of the *'Romani'* from cities in southern Gaul, mentioned in the sources as serving in the royal army of Charlemagne and his successors. Here both the swordsman and his comrade seem to wear iron 'ridge' helmets, one with a nasal, and corselets of moulded leather, complete with Roman-style *pteryges*. (Bibliothèque Nationale de France, BNF Latin 8085, folio 61r; photo courtesy of the Library)

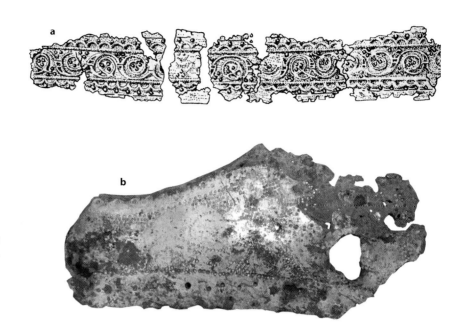

(a) Fragment of Late Roman helmet, probably 5th–6th century, from Greens Norton, Northamptonshire. This gilded copper-alloy strip, 10.4cm (4 ins) long and with a slight convex curvature, seems to be the upper edge of a cheek-guard from a ridge helmet of Alsóheténi typology, with holes on the rim for attaching a lining. An undecorated border along each side, delineated with punched dots, encloses a series of decorative indentations, at least two of them pierced for rivets. The decoration was carried out after the copper was mercury-gilded. (British Museum; PAS NARC-77141, Creative Commons Licence CC BY 4.0)

(b) Fragment of a *Spangenhelm*, 5th–7th century, from Dumfries, Scotland; measuring 6½ ins (16.5cm) long, it is one of several now in the National Museum of Scotland. The embossed copper is covered with gold foil; the central part of the surviving embossed decoration shows a stylized running vine-scroll, as found on other surviving helmets of this type throughout Europe. (Drawing by Andrea Salimbeti, ex-Scott, 1965)

OPPOSITE
Post-Roman copper-alloy *squama* from Rutland, probably 7th century. Small, thin, and originally probably gilded, this appears to be part of a simplified sub-Roman scale armour corselet. (PASLEIC-2ADAA4; Creative Commons Licence CC BY 4.0)

Spangenhelm and *Bandenhelm* types, together with the adoption of Anglo-Saxon and Carolingian models.

Armour and shields

The wealthiest had heavy iron ringmail or scale armours. Following the Late Roman style, Breton shields in the 5th century were round and convex, made of three layers of poplar planks crossed and glued together. Both sides were covered with thin, glued-on rawhide, and the rim was reinforced with a stitched leather band. Shields had a central wooden or metallic grip inside a protruding boss, and usually secondary leather straps for carrying or slinging. The *deigmata* (shield blazons) used by the early Bretons were inherited from Late Roman units stationed in the area (e.g., see under Plate B2). Black or another dark colour was later adopted, and the poem *Armes Prydein* evokes the 'dark armies' of the Armoricans. Two bosses from the Lavret burials roughly correspond to the Walsum type, of mainly Rhenish and Frankish distribution.

Weapons

In the 5th- to early 6th centuries Armoricans and other sub-Roman Gallic warriors probably used organic-hilted swords like those from Namur (see Samson), or resembling Behmer's Types 1 or 5; several Type 1 examples from Cumbria have hilts of horn. Examples from the 7th and 8th centuries follow Merovingian and Anglo-Saxon models, but we cannot exclude local variations.

The 5th-century burials at Saint-Marcel (Morbihan) in southern Brittany yielded no fewer than six knives corresponding to the *culter venatorius* of the Late Roman army, and examples of the *francisca* in the necropolis confirm the presence of Frankish *foederati*.

Late Roman spear types might be used, like the Mamertus example in the Musée Dobrée de Nantes. Armorican tactics were characterized by the employment of light, highly mobile cavalry armed with missile weapons such

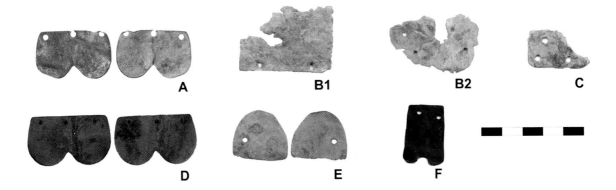

A   **B1**   **B2**   **C**

D   **E**   **F**

as *lanceolae* (javelins), of which heads were recovered at Lavret. The elite had the time for intensive practice, acquiring notable skill in their use from the saddle. The 9th-century Breton history of King Judicael (590–652) praises his expertise, and Emil le Noir (Ch III) describes King Murman holding several javelins in his hand at once.

The favourite weapons of the warrior were personalized with a name (e.g. Arthur's sword Excalibur/*Caledfwlch*, the 'hard-breaching'). The 9th-century Frankish chronicler Reginon de Prum also writes that each trophy of war presented to Charlemagne in 799 by Guy de Bretagne 'was inscribed [with] the name of the chief to whom the weapon belonged'.

Late Roman *squamae* from 5th-century scale armours, found in various British locations.
(A) from Rotherham
(B1 & 2) from Preston Capes
(C) from West Haddon
(D) from North Yorkshire
(E) from Nottinghamshire
(F) from Northumberland
(Creative Commons Licence CC BY 4.0)

Horse equipment

The *Gorchan* or praise-poem of Judicael describes his retainers' steeds as decorated with precious *phalerae*. Breton cavalry was famous, and horses had a fundamental importance; a 7th-century Breton law provided that the man who found a lost horse was entitled to one-third of its value. Sources from the 7th to 9th centuries set the price of a horse at 20 *solidi*, the same as for a *lorica* and four times that of a sword (*Gesta Sanctorum Rotonensium* I, col.238; Cartulaire de Redon, charte 157). An exceptional pair of spurs, with fabric thongs, were found in the apparently 7th-century Grave 26 at Lavret, but have been interpreted as a later burial.

Military dress

A 'Phrygian'-shaped cap was a usual military headgear, alone or as padding under a helmet; it was associated with the cult of Mithras, which long had many devotees among Roman soldiers. This cap was clearly used widely in the Western as well as the Eastern Empire: it is seen in the *Vergilius Romanus* miniatures; worn by Gallo-Roman soldiers on the ivory buckle-

(See caption opposite.)

Three images of a shield boss, plus handle fragments, from Lincolnshire; dated to 410–575, Dickinson's Group 4 classification. With a total depth of *c*.95mm (3¾ ins), and a 30mm-wide (1¼-in) flat flange, this *umbo* is hemispherical on the inside but has an external 'step' at the base, and a 'button' apex. A surviving iron rivet in the flange indicates shield boards *c*.10mm (⅓ in) thick. The fragments of the internal handle reinforcement measure 63 x 17mm (2½ x ⅔ ins), and one preserves impressions of wood grain. (PASNLM-388C8D; Creative Commons Licence CC BY 4.0).

plate of the 'Caesarius belt'; and was still in use by the later Anglo-Saxons (Ms. Cotton; Claudius, B.IV, BL).

Male clothing for the well-to-do consisted of a long-sleeved Late Roman-style decorated *tunica manicata*, worn over a knee-length T-shaped *camision*, usually of white or a neutral colour, with narrow sleeves to the wrist. The tunic neck was straight or rounded, and the skirt was slit at each side for ease of movement. Cloaks might be of either circular or semi-circular *chlamys* type, or the rectangular *sagum*, and reddish-orange is the dominant colour depicted in the *Vergilius Romanus* miniatures. The Gallo-Romans continued to use a Late Roman hooded cape (*cocullus*; HF,VII,39). Legs were protected either by long, tight trousers, possibly with gaiters, worn with *campagi*-type shoes (enclosing heels and toes, and laced over the open instep); or by shorter trousers (or none at all) with puttees and *calcei* (closed, laced ankle-boots).

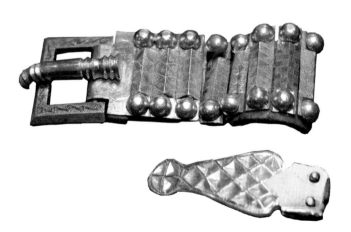

Belt buckle with *alpha* and *omega* decorations, eight silvered stiffeners, and chip-carved strap-end; *c*.430, from the Traprain Law hoard, Edinburgh. This type of buckle is typical of Rome's Danubian provinces, but finds have also been made at Point-de-Buis and Saint-Marcel in Brittany, suggesting the transfer of troops. Traces of leather were found mineralized to these fittings. (National Museum of Scotland; photo courtesy of Matt Bunker)

In Britain, northern Gaul and particularly in 5th-century Armorica military accoutrements, such as decorated belts, and 'crossbow' *fibulae* to fasten the cloak, were clearly status symbols for the wealthy and their close followers. Various accessories and jewellery included torques, bracelets and rings. From the end of the 4th century, burials of Germanic soldiers in Brittany begin to include Roman-style *fibulae*. Pennanular brooches (i.e. shaped as an incomplete circle) are shown in the *Vergilius Romanus* miniatures, and are supported by burial finds from Bénouville, Normandy. Spectacular

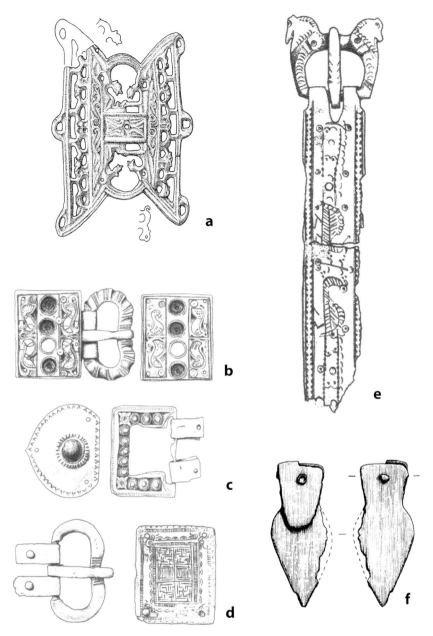

Early post-Roman British military equipment fittings. *(Left, top to bottom:)* **(a)** Gilded copper-alloy equal-arm brooch; Collingbourne Ducis, Wiltshire, mid-5th–early 6th century. **(b–d)** Shallow chip-carved belt sets: **(b)** from Alfriston, Sussex, Grave 17; **(c)** from Highdown, Sussex; **(d)** from Morningthorpe, Norfolk. *(Right, top to bottom:)* **(e)** Buckle from Stanwix, Cumbria. **(f)** Belt end from Cirencester, Gloucestershire, early 5th century. (Drawings by Andrea Salimbeti, ex-McWhirr, 1986; Inker, 2000; & Blair-Hamerow, 2005)

recent recoveries from a cemetery at Saint-Marcel include 5th- to early 6th-century military belts and weapons showing 'quoit-brooch' style metalwork. This is believed to be a hybrid of Romano-Celtic and Germanic traditions characteristic of both southern Britain and Armorica, confirming their connection. Examples have also been found in other burials in northern Gaul, spread between Finistère and the Somme.

The Bretons were apparently visibly distinguishable from their enemies. During a 6th-century war against Guntram's Burgundian Franks, the Bretons' Saxon allies from Bayeux cut their hair short according to the Breton (i.e. Roman) style, and adopted clothes in the Breton fashion (HF, X, 9).

BRITISH WARLORD ARMIES

Gildas writes that the Romans left Britain deprived of soldiers and military supplies, but before they left they armed the Britons and provided *exemplaria instituendorum armorum* (perhaps meaning military manuals?). The historian Zosimus states that when the usurper Constantine III, with his British general Gerontius (Custennin, 'Gereint' in Welsh legend), withdrew the last field units to Gaul in *c*.407, old men and boys were left to defend the island in local militias (though this may have been a deliberately scathing reference to hereditary border units).

One of the main problems in reconstructing Romano-British warriors is not the lack of military items among the archaeology, but its cultural identification. Due to the influence of Christianity, personal grave goods such as armour and weapons were no longer interred with the owners except in the cases of pagan mercenaries. Since Saxons retained these practices, most military artefacts recovered are identified as Germanic. Brittonic material culture is much less well known, and (as already argued) Roman provincial and Germanic cultures increasingly overlapped during the 5th–6th centuries, so it is possible that many 'Anglo-Saxon' burials were in fact those of Britons. Roman military equipment mingled with inherited native British weaponry, and with imported luxury items like the Germanic brooches of Saxon *foederati*. The early Anglo-Saxon cemetery at Kempston near Bedford has produced both Roman finds and early Germanic metalwork, suggesting a mingling of Britons and Saxons.

Leslie Alcock has highlighted the overwhelming evidence for the continuity of maritime traffic between western Britain and the continental Empire in the 5th–6th centuries, proving that the Saxon conquest of eastern Britain did not isolate the Romano-British. Besides domestic and utilitarian goods, imports included military artefacts. Over time, all these influences probably merged to produce a 'post-Roman British' style.

Helmets

Only two fragmentary sub-Roman helmets survive from 6th-century Britain: a *Spangenhelm*, and part of a helmet of possible Alsóhéteni typology. The Roman heavy cavalry 'ridge' helmets of Berkasovo and Budapest typology, covered with silver or gilt sheet and highly decorated with inlaid glass or semi-precious gemstones, may still have been in use in the 'Arthurian' period.

1

2

5th-century 'quoit' brooches, from (**1**) Sarre and (**2**) Howletts, both in Kent. (British Museum, inv 1893 & 0601; photos Raffaele D'Amato, courtesy of the Museum)

 BATTLE OF CATRAETH, AD *c.* 590–600: HEROES OF *Y GODODDIN*

(1) Cynon
The poem describes the aristocratic heroes leading divisions of the expedition as 'gold-collared', i.e. distinguished by gold neck torques. The expression *Eurar vur caer* also seems to refer to gilded armours; the scale armour here is reconstructed from the Rutland fragment. Many warriors (e.g. Cadfannan) are described as armed with several spears; and some 'planted shafts in battle' against the enemy's front rank. Cynon is also armed with a 'keen-edged blade' and his shield is painted white. Note the richness of his clothing and accoutrements.

(2) Owein ap Marro
This famous *loricatus* wears a fine coat of iron ringmail; there are references to 'three mail-clad war-bands' (*Tri llu llurugawc* (YG XVIII), and to 'glittering armours' (*llurugeu clear*, XXXIII;

genhyn llurugogyon, LIX). His *Spangenhelm* is reconstructed from fragments from Dumfries; forearm protection, and woollen clothing in red and white, are again mentioned in the poem. Horse trappings in *Y Gododdin* are described as black or dark brown (XXXIII), and the spurs (*ethy*) as gilded – a feature repeated in a poem describing the son of Llywarch Hen.

(3) Erthai
'Beautiful he burned in gold and purple, riding his well-fed horses'. Silk and dark garments are mentioned for the elite warriors (*gwisgyssant eu gwrym*). Clasps in the Sutton Hoo Saxon ship burial have been identified by Gamber as fittings from a Roman-style muscled armour in leather, possibly of Gallo-Roman origin. If this is true, it is highly probable that such armours were also worn by sub-Roman leaders in Britain. We reconstruct the helmet as of Roman derivation, but basically resembling the Sutton Hoo shape.

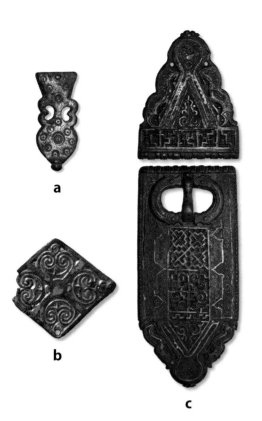

a

b

c

5th–6th century Romano-British military belt fittings:
(a) 5th-century copper-alloy strap end, with Late Roman ring-and-dot decoration, from Haslingfield, Cambridgeshire.
(b) Unprovenanced 6th-century gilded copper-alloy belt mount, of lozenge shape with palmette decoration.
(c) Buckle mounts of the 6th-century 'Mucking belt', from that village on the Thames in Essex. Decorated in 'quoit-brooch' style, these mounts, measuring 10.1cm x 4.8cm (4 x 1¾ ins), suggest co-operative contact between Britons and Saxons. (British Museum inv 1970, 0406.26.b; photos courtesy of Brett Hammond & Steven Pollington)

Among the Richborough Collection are seven oval and circular black and pale-blue glass cameo gems. Some of them are too big to come from finger-rings, but appear to be identical in form, size and colour to those on the Berkasovo and Budapest helmets.

A passage in *The Dream of Rhonawby* from the *Mabinogion* describes three horsemen, wearing on their heads: '... A golden helmet with precious... stones in it, on top of the helmet an image of a yellow-red leopard, with two crimson-red stones in its head... A golden helmet with magic sapphires in it, and on top of the helmet an image of a yellow-red lion, its foot-long, flame-red tongue sticking out of its mouth, and crimson-red, poisonous eyes in its head... A shining helmet of yellow latten [brass] with shining crystals in it, and on top of the helmet an image of a griffon with magic stones in its head'. Lion and griffon motifs are visible on various decorated Roman helmets from the 3rd century onward. The silhouette of helmets depicted in the 5th–6th century Ostrogothic treasure of Domagnano suggests that they formed crests.

We know very little about other helmet types employed, but logically they too should have been of Late Roman styles. The 5th-century Burgh Castle *Spangenhelm* specimen is of heavy 'ridge' typology; it is made of four iron segments fixed together with a crest and two reinforcing bands, using copper-alloy rivets, with surviving elements of a brow-band and cheek-pieces. The ridge was made of iron folded out at the bottom to produce flanges, and riveted to the segmental plates. The Shorwell helmet, dated to 500–550, is a sturdy, utilitarian fighting helmet made from eight riveted iron bands and segments; it was found in the grave of a Saxon warrior, but is closely similar to Late Roman helmets from Trivières in Hainault, Belgium (see photo on page 14), and Bretzenheim in the German Rhineland. Under the helmet a cap would have been worn as padding, and in the 5th century this may perhaps have still copied the 'pillbox' *pileus Pannonicus* of the Late Roman army.

Body armour

Ringmail was probably the commonest armour used by elites such as heavy cavalry. It is mentioned in the *The Dream of Rhonawby*, and, at least in the 5th–early 6th centuries, would still have been of typical Roman construction – alternating rows of complete and riveted rings. Fragments of scale armour were found in levels dated to c.400–410, and, like ringmail, well cared-for metal scales would last for several generations. Over time, however, craftsmen with the skills to manufacture and repair metal armour would have become increasingly scarce, so such expensive protection would have become limited to small elites. We may suppose that cheaper and more easily-worked organic replacements were adopted, since materials such as leather, horn and felt had already been used for centuries in Roman armies.

While leather armours for men have not survived, in the Middle East examples of Roman leather horse armour have. Many researchers dismiss the plentiful Late Antique iconography showing 'muscled' leather armour as a mere artistic convention, although it was still being depicted in 9th-century Carolingian manuscripts alongside metal equipment that is confirmed by archaeology. Meanwhile, experimental reconstructions by Gansser-Burchdart, and by Dan Shadrake of the 'Britannia' group, have proved that boiled, shaped and moulded leather can resist thrusts as effectively as mild steel. Simpler 'soft' protections, such as hide or padded fabric corselets, would have been cheaper and easier to produce in quantity.

Shields

The circular or oval shield of larger dimensions used by the Late Roman army was certainly retained in the 5th–6th centuries, either convex or flat in section. The *Vergilius Romanus* codex shows bosses close to the Rhenen-Vermand type, of which examples were found in a 4th to 5th-century context near the Saxon Shore fort at Richborough, Kent. Some have a 'button' apex, similar to later Anglo-Saxon and Merovingian specimens. An isolated *umbo* of this type from Lincolnshire may be a battlefield relic from as late as *c.*575.

Certainly during the 5th century, sub-Roman *Britanni* on both sides of the Channel, especially those descended from Roman soldiers, would have retained the painted shield devices of units formerly stationed in Britain. These were listed as including the *Secundani Britones Juniores*, the *Numerus Fortensium*, the *Militum Tungrecanorum*, the *Militum Turnacensium*, the *Equites Dalmati Branodunensium*, the *Prima Cohors Vetasiorum*, the *Numeri Abulcorum* and *Exploratorum*, and the *Equites Stablesiani Gariannonensium*. Surviving copies of the *Notitia Dignitatum* illustrate some but far from all of the corresponding shield blazons.

Alongside military *deigmata*, the Christian Romano-Britons probably used Christian symbols to distinguish themselves from the pagan Saxons, who converted to Christianity only after 616. These were probably very similar to the *Chi-Ro* and crosses engraved on Romano-British monuments of the 6th and 7th centuries. A medallion from London shows a possible shield emblem, representing two birds facing one another each side of a Christian cross mounted on steps.

The *Annales Cambriae* describe Arthur at the battle of Badon Hill, 'carrying the cross of Christ on his shoulders for three days and three nights' (AC cw125.3, a72.1, b546.1). The Old Welsh words for shoulder *(scuid)* and shield *(scuit)* were easily confused. It is also possible that this was a conventional phrase for carrying a slung shield; there is another reference (HB 50) to Arthur wearing an image of the Virgin Mary upon his shoulders *(super humeros suos)* at the battle of Gurnion.

Military belts

For the reasons explained at the beginning of this chapter, the users of most recovered Late Roman-style military belt-fittings dated to the 5th or 6th

Further details of 5th-century Late Roman sword and scabbard from Grave 31 at Brighthampton, Oxfordshire, which show both Romano-Celtic 'repeat-pattern' and Germanic 'animal' decorative elements. See also page 5. (Photos courtesy of Matt Bunker)

(Left) The 'Catterick buckle' from Yorkshire, first half of 5th century. (British Museum; photo Raffaele D'Amato, courtesy of the Museum) (Centre & right) Details of the contemporary 'Richborough dagger' from Kent. (ex-Bushe-Fox, 1949)

centuries are indistinguishable between sub-Roman Britons, Germanic *foederati* or Saxon invaders. Archaeologists have nevertheless classified various styles after their find-sites; for instance, the Catterick style in copper alloy or silvered, from 8.5 to 14cm wide (3⅓–5½ ins), with an openwork plate showing dolphins flanking a temple. Among the most striking sub-Roman examples are the Traprain Law belt fittings, and the Mucking *cingulum* decorated in the 'quoit-brooch' style. The latter was essentially a hybrid style of metalwork apparently developed in Kent in the late 4th and early 5th centuries, which combined continental Late Roman with distinctively British (perhaps Dubonnic) influences.

Standards

According to the earliest legendary sources, Arthur's standard-bearer was termed the *Gwres ap Rheged*, and carried the banner of the Red Dragon of Britannia into battle (presumably a late-Roman 'windsock' flag with a metal head in the shape of a *draco*). In the HB (42), the *rufus draco* of Britannia is opposed to the white *albus draco* of the Saxons.

Sub-Roman British spearheads, 5th–6th century, from various locations in London, Middlesex, Surrey, Berkshire and Leicestershire. Note the very distinctive cross-sections. (Drawings by Andrea Salimbeti, ex-Swanton)

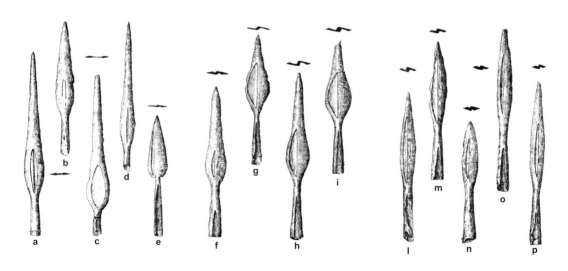

Large, fine-grained whetstone, c.850, from Wales. It is of squared cross-section, smooth on all four sides, and this quality suggests that it may have been used to sharpen weapons. That possibility is supported by the copper-alloy ferrule, apparently once silvered, in the form of a helmet with nose-, neck- and cheek-guards. The nose-guard is decorated with punched lines and ring-and-dot decoration. At the apex is a ring, perhaps recalling the Late Roman helmet from Deir-El Medina in Egypt. (Photo courtesy of National Museum of Wales, WASC 14.2)

Weapons:

Spears

In the 5th century throwing-spears were of Late Roman typology. Near Kenchester, Herefordshire, two broad barbed javelin heads of late 4th to early 5th-century date were found, comparable with finds from Carvoran and South Shields in the Wall zone. One is socketed, and 5cm (2 ins) long.

Sub-Roman finds from the late 5th and early 6th century are very scarce. Plain leaf-bladed examples with fairly long sockets and slightly rounded tips, suitable for cavalry or infantry use, were found in Germanic graves, and another comes from Liddington Castle hillfort (one of the possible locations of Badon Hill). A few early Germanic spearheads and arrowheads have been recovered from the hillforts of Cadbury (Devonshire), Dolebury and Worlebury (both in Somerset), and Hod Hill and Badbury (Dorset). These may perhaps be Romano-British war-booty, or else indicative of the presence of Saxon mercenaries. Three other specimens came from Coygan Camp, a promontory fort in the kingdom of Dyfed. Romano-British 5th–6th century spearheads, originally classified by Swanton as

Iron leaf-shaped spearhead, c.700, from Buiston Crannog, Ayrshire, in the ancient kingdom of Strathclyde. Measuring 8½ ins (21.5cm) long, with a midrib and pronounced medial thickening, it is more robust than most known spears from Scottish and Irish sites, and is probably a thrusting weapon. The socket has two bands of triple grooves, which may once have held silver or copper-alloy wire inlays. (Photo courtesy of National Museum of Scotland)

45

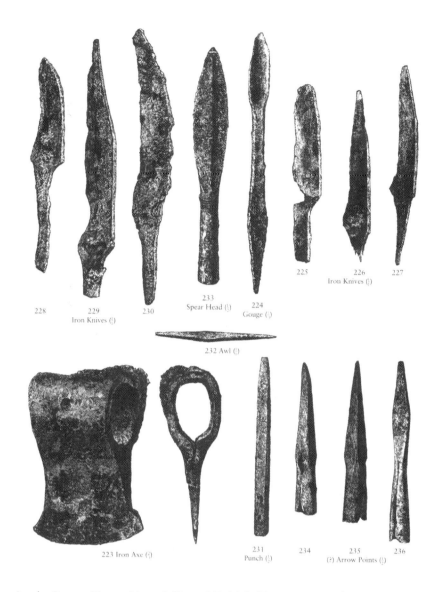

Tools and weapons from Buiston Crannog. The most common iron personal items found on Celtic sites are small, single-edged, tanged knife blades of tapering triangular cross-section. They usually measure between 1½ and 5¼ ins (38–132mm) long, so their identification as either domestic tools or weapons is arbitrary. This axe is usually regarded as a carpenter's tool, without excluding a military use. (ex-Munro, 1903)

228　　229　　230　　233　　224
Iron Knives (⅓)　Spear Head (⅓)　Gouge (⅓)

225　226　227
Iron Knives (⅓)

232 Awl (⅓)

223 Iron Axe (⅓)　　231 Punch (⅓)　234　235 (?) Arrow Points (⅓)　236

Anglo-Saxon Types I1 and I2 and British Type K1, are found across the future extent of Wessex (see page 44); having no parallels in Scandinavia or continental Europe, they may suggest the presence of Jutes in cooperation with the British. This interpretation is supported by the appearance of such spearheads in graves that also contain 'quoit-brooch' style items suggesting a mixed context. Later but associated spearheads with fullered blades are found across the same areas of Hampshire as Swanton's Type I1, and in both the West Country and the North.

Swords

Spatha swords of the 5th and 6th centuries are well documented, but the early presence of Saxon *foederati* and the consequent Germanic imports of swords, baldric buckles and other accessories make it problematic to identify any distinctively British type. The later dominance of Germanic-style long, parallel-sided *spathae* with Saxon and Frankish styles of hilt is highly probable. The sword from Grave 34 at Brighthampton, Oxfordshire, with a chape decorated in 'quoit-brooch' style, may be a transitional example. Copper-alloy scabbard slides, mouths and chapes from Blacknall Field, Pewsey, Wiltshire were found in Anglo-Saxon contexts but also show Romano-Celtic influence. Such items may also show decoration in Frankish styles recalling examples from the Rhineland and northern Gaul.

Daggers and knives

Some copper-alloy sheath fittings found in Anglo-Saxon contexts, such as one from the 6th-century Grave 22 at Brighthampton, were decorated in a late Romano-British style. It may perhaps be specifically Dubonnic, since the find was made on the probable edge of Dubonnic tribal militia territory. The dagger was probably, by the standards of the period, an exceptionally fine piece with intricately decorated fittings, very different from other finds with fittings made only from organic materials. From Cadbury Castle came two (possibly four) left-handed iron knives similar to examples from a 5th–6th century fort at Dinas Powys.

Trigger-nut from a crossbow, and bolt heads, from Buiston Crannog. The pivoting nut is rather crudely carved from deer antler. The socketed iron bolts have pyramidal heads, one of them heavy and of tapering square cross-section. (Photo courtesy of National Museum of Scotland)

Axes

Side-axes with small heads and short hafts were a practical weapon amongst the Romano-British. A small *francisca* throwing-axe of the late 5th or early 6th century was found at Wroxeter, Shropshire, perhaps suggesting the presence of Frankish troops in Romano-British service. An iron axe-hammer was found on the site of Cadbury Camp, and a socketed axe with triangular blade at Dinas Powys.

The 9th-century 'Drosten Stone' from St Vigeans, Arbroath, is the most important known iconographic evidence for the use of the crossbow in post-Roman Britain. While the carving depicts a wild-animal hunt, it is inconceivable that such an effective weapon was not also used in warfare. (Photo Raffaele D'Amato, courtesy of St Vigeans Museum)

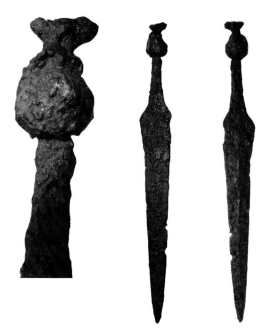

Cavalry equipment

The mobility of early campaigns between the Britons and Saxons suggests that some forces were mounted. It does not prove that they engaged solely as cavalry, but it is likely that British forces were capable of fighting from horseback. Gildas calls Cuneglassus (Cynlas Goch) of Gwynned 'a horseman among many', and writes evocatively of cavalry warfare. Zoomorphic prick spurs and belt equipment at Cirencester are part of finds that appear to date from *c.*365 into the 5th century. These spurs were more associated with barbarian warriors than Roman cavalry, but both used them in Britain. The gear of Romano-British cavalry of the period was probably of Late Roman type, but Celto-British military culture was centred on the skills of mounted fighters. A mixture of small, sturdy native highland ponies and imported Roman cavalry horses would have been ideal for the rugged terrain of the north, for instance in Rheged, and may have contributed to that kingdom's domination of its neighbours. In some tales Arthur and his horsemen are reputed to have ridden black horses, perhaps a reference to the usually black or dark brown fell-ponies of the high moors.

Romano-British double-edged iron dagger, 5th–6th century, from Coygan Camp, Carmarthenshire. Overall length 11¾ ins (29.8 cm); the slender leaf-shaped blade has a slight median ridge on both sides. The tang passed through an iron ball pommel before being burred. Traces of wood, animal pelt and wool from the scabbard were identifiable on the blade. (Photo courtesy of Matt Bunker)

POST-ROMAN KINGDOMS

Both large-scale manufacture of equipment and weapons, and imports from the Mediterranean world, must have declined over time (although excavations in 1974/75 in the 'Old North' revealed that long-distance trading in quality goods continued into the 7th and 8th centuries). A sort of 'cottage industry' of craftsmen remained in some sheltered hubs, and in regions beyond the reach of the Anglo-Saxon culture Late Roman styles probably survived for a time, but gradually the models for items of military equipment became pre-Roman British, Pictish, Irish, and Saxon.

G **BRITISH POST-ROMAN KINGDOMS, 6th–8th CENTURY**
(1) Crossbowman, *Alt Clut* **(Strathclyde), AD 658–752**
This warrior is reconstructed from various sources in modern Scotland. The hooded, fringed cloak is from the 'Orkney hood', carbon-dated to 615 at the latest but apparently repurposed later, and reconstructed by Jacqui Wood. The shoes, fighting knife, axe, buckle, and crossbow bolts are from Buiston Crannog, Ayrshire, and the crossbow from the Drosten Stone, Arbroath. Crossbows already appear in Roman-related iconography of the 3rd century (e.g. relief in Museum Crozatier, Le Puy); they seem to have been of elementary design, with a rising-peg trigger and a pivoting release-nut carved from horn.
(2) Archer, Rheged (Cumbria), 7th century
Reconstructed mainly from the Ruthwell Cross, we have given him padded fabric 'soft armour', and a helmet based on the 7th-century Anglo-Saxon so-called 'Pioneer' example from

Wollaston, Northamptonshire with its hanging mail neck protection but without its wild-boar crest. His bow is taken from Late Roman sources, and the pin-brooch from northern England.
(3) Sub-Roman chieftain; Vindolanda, Hadrian's Wall, 6th century
A northern British leader such as Brigomaglos, in the old military territory of *Britannia Secunda,* might have looked like this. The helmet shows an iron frame over a brown leather head-piece. The oval shield, based on Late Roman examples, bears the Christian symbols found in Vindolanda, on the white background mentioned in *Y Gododdin.* The spear is copied from a Romano-British example found in Berkshire, and the red woollen cloak resembles a Roman *sagum.* The great majority of the armour worn by the Britons ('Welsh') is likely to have been made of leather and/or other perishable organic material.

Sub-Roman *spatha*, 5th–7th century, from Lagore Crannog, Co. Meath, Ireland; a *gladius* blade of classic Pompeii shape was also recovered from this site. The presence of such typically Roman weapons, imported or looted from the British mainland, suggests that local Romano-British craftsmen were stll manufacturing them. (Copyright National Museum of Ireland, inv KA386)

Helmets

Given the difficulty of producing and working high-quality metal, we may suspect that helmets became limited to elites; *Y Gododdin* specifically mentions booty collected from the battlefield. Helmets were probably still derived from basic Late Roman designs such as the *Spangenhelm*; in *Y Gododdin* (XI) we find mention of 'helmets divided into four parts', and red plumes. (In the *Elegy on Cynddylan* the late 6th-century princely bard of Rheged, Llywarch Hen, describes himself as having worn yellow plumes.)

The richly decorated 7th-century helmet of an Anglo-Saxon king from the ship burial at Sutton Hoo is clearly influenced by Late Roman-style 'ridge' models, though not in its actual manufacture. Some 6th to 7th-century sub-Roman helmets may have followed if not its rich Germanic decoration, then at least its basic components – the iron bowl with a central ridge or crest, with pendant cheek- and neck-guards. This is suggested by the archer's helmet depicted on the mid-7th-century Ruthwell Cross, carved in an area where Strathclyde, the Rheged Britons, and the Northumbrian and Bernician Saxons fought constantly. A large 8th to 9th-century whetstone from Wales may provide evidence for late Romano-British helmets, and is the only Welsh depiction found so far. Its ferrule takes the form of a helmet with nose-, cheek- and neck-guards – perhaps an embryonic local development of the Coppergate-type Northumbrian helmet as found in York.

Armour

Y Gododdin describes armoured riders: 'Warriors went to Catraeth... a host of horsemen in dark blue armour, with shields, spear shafts... shining *loricae* and swords' ('blue' presumably imeaning iron, perhaps even lacquered?). The terminology for armour is open to a variety of interpretations. The many

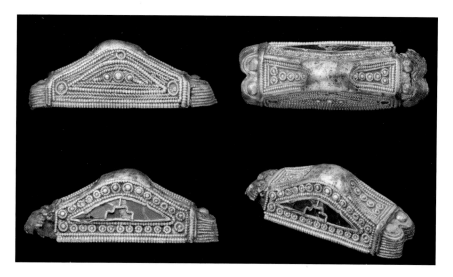

Silver sword-pommel cap inlaid with garnet, *c.*600–650. This was found near Bresford, north-east Wales, in the borderlands between the ancient kingdoms of Powys and Mercia. (St Fagans Wales Is Gallery, inv 2008.17H; photo courtesy of National Museum of Wales)

references in *Y Gododdin* use two terms: *seirch* (XXIV) and, more regularly, *lluric*. *Seirch* can be translated either as 'armour' or 'harness'(LXXXIX), and may thus refer to leather sword-straps or horse-harness, described as dark (XXXIII). But sometimes it clearly refers to an armoured warrior (*seirchyawc*) or armoured spearman (*seirchyawc saphwyawc*), or indicates war-gear (*seirchyawr*). *Lluric* derives from the Latin *lorica*, and thus refers to mail or scale armour, or possibly to leather protection. The *Triads* mention Lludd Llurigog ('Llud of the Breastplate'), which suggests that this hero's armour was considered remarkable.

The use of ringmail undoubtedly continued in Britain through the 6th century and beyond, but following the collapse of any centralized manufacturing system it would surely have been limited to the military elite, like the heroes of *Y Gododdin*. The Anglo-Saxon Sutton Hoo find included fragments of mail, with links alternately butted and fixed with copper-alloy rivets.

Limb armour and gauntlets are mentioned (e.g. YG, I, 44). The finds of splinted leg or arm armour in 6th–8th century Vendel graves in Sweden allow us to suppose that some Romano-Britons may have used similar protection in this period of cultural cross-influences.

Shields

The most frequent words for shield, *sgwyd/ ysgwyt/ yscuit*, are derived from the Latin *scutum*. Other terms used are *cylchwy* and *rhodawg/rhodawr* (circular shield), or round war-buckler (*rodawr-gwasgarawc*). They seem not to have been very strong, since they are often described as being 'shattered', 'splintered', or 'not solid'.

In *Y Gododdin* the shields are described as light and broad (V), generally coloured white (XI), and sometimes decorated with gold (XXIV, XXIX). Mentions of 'chalked' and 'ice-bright' shields may perhaps refer to the Late Roman technique of applying paint directly onto wet plaster (i.e. the 'fresco' method). In such a case, adding earth- or vegetable-colours to a wet ground-chalk surface would have brightened and intensified the colours. Metallic fittings have been found mainly in Anglo-Saxon graves, but not exclusively so; in Dinas Powys similar shield ornaments were found, together with belt fittings of distinctive Kentish type. When not in use shields were slung from the flank of the war-horse (YG, VI, L).

Weapons

According to *Y Gododdin,* each warrior certainly had more than one spear, and it mentions them more often than swords. For instance, Eithinyn is described as 'a spear-thrusting lord, laughing in war' (XXXVIII, Clancy version). The poem uses more than 15 terms in association with spears, and this diversity continues in later sources, embracing both throwing and thrusting weapons.

There are frequent references to the 'scattering' of spears between armies, and to 'showered shafts in the front rank of the fray, in the javelin fight'. In common usage

(A) Angled images of fragment from a scabbard chape from Llanbedrgoch, Anglesey, and **(B)** scabbard fitting from Goldcliff, Gwent; both 6th–7th century. In the *Lives* of Welsh saints, we read of fine swords being granted in reparation or in exchange for land rights, and laws made provision for the greater value of decorated swords and scabbards. (St Fagans Wales Is Gallery, inv SH515813 & 2008.9H; photos courtesy of National Museum of Wales)

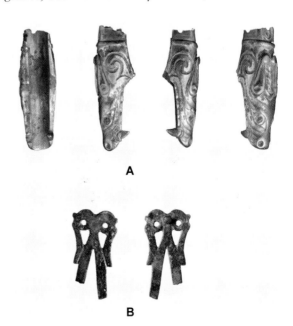

A

B

the Old Welsh word translated as 'scattering' refers to a farmer casting seed, suggesting that the individual warrior carried a clutch of javelins. Koch's translation describes Marchleu, a warrior who 'scattered his ashwood [spears] from the four clefts of his hand'. Hand-to-hand fighting with spears is also mentioned: 'He ripped and pierced with his spearpoints, Deep in blood he butchered with blades' (YG, XIV). Spears are described as long, coloured yellow or brown, usually of ash (XVIII) or holly wood. The heads are sometimes 'square-pointed' (in section), with sockets of dark-blue metal.

Nearly every warrior named in poems carries a sword (*gledyf*). They are described as bright blue, shining, with sharpened blades used for swift, slashing blows, so were probably the long *spathae* inherited from the Late Roman army. At least two sub-Roman swords, a *spatha* and a *gladius*, have been found in Ireland, dated to between the 6th and 8th century. The *spatha* long continued in use by both Anglo-Saxons and sub-Roman Britons. Two studies of numerous Anglo-Saxon skeletons in the Heronbridge cemetery, probably associated with the early 7th-century battle of Chester, suggest that most were killed by slashing sword-blows. Two skeletons exhumed in 2004 were certainly killed by sword-cuts to the head, although one also seems to have been stabbed through the lower abdomen with a narrow-bladed weapon.

In *Y Gododdin*, axes (LXXXIV, *bwyllyadeu*, 'the stroke of battle-axe') and daggers (*gyllell*) are mentioned as secondary weapons, carried by the elite and the common soldier alike. Healed skull wounds on one of the Heronbridge skeletons are thought to have been caused by a blunt weapon, possibly a hammer.

The use of bows in hunting, and so presumably in warfare, is attested on the Ruthwell Cross from the Solway Firth, dated slightly before 660, and on the Pictish Shandwick Stone from Easter Ross. Evidence for the use of the crossbow is provided by a single 5th to 6th-century bolt from South Cadbury, and others, with a trigger-nut, from Buiston Crannog, Ayrshire. These finds

confirm the famous representation of a crossbowman on the Drosten Stone (St Vigeans, Arbroath).

Cavalry warfare

The breakdown of order in Britain following the departure of the Roman army might have disrupted the systematic breeding of cavalry horses. However, the possibility that the Brittonic nobility continued to possess superior horses is suggested by Taliesin's poem on the battle of Gwen Ystrad, in which Urien's Pictish enemies are mocked for their small ponies *(kaffon)* in comparison with the fine steeds of the Britons. Passages in *Y Gododdin* support this theory, by references to stalling and grain-feeding, and to Guaurthur being a breeder of horses, and in the *Stanzas on Graves* there is a mention of warhorses being specially bred. While perhaps unsuited to heavy armoured cavalry, even the native British ponies were sturdy enough for most other purposes. Saddles and spurs are mentioned, but not stirrups.

Mounted warriors formed the core (at least) of the expedition to Catraeth, fighting both in the saddle and dismounted. Heavy cavalry may have made close-order charges against formed bodies of the enemy, but apparently using spears as missile weapons rather than couched lances, before closing with the sword. Nonetheless, the impact of the charge is emphasized. Traditions preserved in the *Historia Brittonum* express the belief that the battle of Badon Hill was decided by a British charge: 'The twelfth battle was at Badon Hill, and in it 916 men fell in one day from a single charge of Arthur's'. In the aftermath the *loricati* give no quarter to the Saxons, whom they pursue and 'cut down like rushes'.

There are suggestions in *Y Gododdin* that at Catraeth the force was drawn up in tactical units rather than making a disorganized rush at the enemy, and, despite the emphasis on cavalry, that the heroes also fought on foot. While this may have been because they were unhorsed in battle, it is also possible that an infantry screen was used to protect the cavalry.

Military dress

Belts were a specifically military status symbol in the Late Imperial period, and continued as such in the surviving parts of the Empire. There was a growing militarisation of male dress, but whether every young man with the latest horse-head belt-buckle was a soldier or member of a militia is unclear. The overlapping and merging of material cultures, already emphasized, usually makes the differentiation of graves between Romano-Britons and Germanics highly problematic. For example, while a high-status Briton buried at Collingbourne Ducis, Wiltshire, had a 5th or 6th-century inlaid buckle at his waist and a Romano-British brooch at his shoulder, three British penannular brooches worn singly at the shoulder in Romano-British fashion were found in Saxon graves at Morningthorpe, Norfolk.

Very little is known about male dress specifically of the post-Roman Britons. The basic Late Roman costume (of long-sleeved,

A possibly Romano-British boar's-head *fibula*, c.6th–8th century. This finely-worked silver brooch-pin for fastening cloaks terminates in a head with a ridged mane and tusks, the eyes, 'tail', and three other circular extensions, being set with garnets. A similar example is preserved in the British Museum, inventory PRB 1954.12-6.1. (Private collection; photo courtesy of Timeline Auctions)

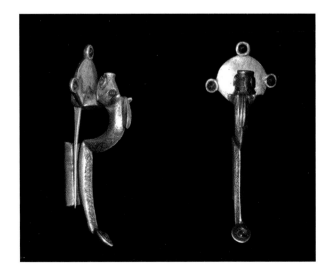

8th-century pennanular brooch from Newton Moor, Vale of Glamorgan. These open-hoop brooch-pins were popular in Wales between the 5th and 9th century; usually made in copper-alloy, in costlier metals they became symbols of rank among the post-Roman aristocracy. This example, with an external hoop diameter of 51mm (c.2 in), partial gilding, gold foil, filigree and two blue glass beads, is the first gilded specimen found in Wales. (National Museum of Wales, acc. no. 92.4H; photo courtesy of the Museum)

knee-length tunic closed by a belt, trousers, and a cloak) certainly survived, with some Germanic additions and new Celtic influences from Ireland. The military costume of the 5th century was probably as described above for the Armoricans. A hint of the use of the Late Roman military 'Pannonian cap' among Romano-Britons and/or Saxon *foederati* is given by the famous seated figurine from the Saxon cemetery at Spong Hill, Norfolk.

The most common fabrics were linen and wool, with some silk from the Roman East probably still arriving until the early 7th century. Cloaks might be of solid colours, or of Celtic chequered weaves, usually fastened on the right shoulder with penannular brooches. Examples of woven chequered wool fabric from the Roman era and later have been found in England and Scotland, such as the important Late Roman example in dark brown and light yellow-brown from Falkirk.

Shoes, in more-or-less fragmentary condition, have occasionally been found. A rather simple example from Buiston Crannog has been

WALES AND THE SOUTH-WEST, 7th–8th CENTURY

(1) Cadwallon of Gwynned, AD 633
We have chosen to reconstruct the great northern Welsh victor Cadwallon (Catguollaunus), 'leader of the hosts of Britain', as a true Late Roman warlord. His muscled cuirass, an echo of Roman commanders, is inspired by Taliesin's mention in the *Cedair Theirn On*, apparently describing Ambrosius Aurelianus 'clad in a legionary *lorica (lleon lluryg)*'. His sword is based on fragments of a magnificent pattern-welded blade found at Gresford, near Wrexham in the Welsh Marches.

(2) Sub-Roman *penteulu*, Dumnonia, 7th century
An important slate found in Tintagel, Cornwall, shows a sub-Roman Dumnonian warrior armed with a sword and small round shield; this forms the basis of our attempted reconstruction of a 'unit commander'. The graffito shows two warriors wearing conical helmets, one apparently of *Spangenhelm* construction, and an armour, here reconstructed

as a copper-alloy *squama* from the Stenton finds, worn over padded protection. His weaponry is copied from that of the Cornish lord's burial at Lowbury Hill. The *Chi-Ro* on his shield is taken from the cross patterns of the Hayle and Phillack stones in Cornwall.

(3) *Toisech*, Powys, c.750
An elite commander, this mail-clad warrior serves King Elisedd ap Gwylog of Powys. The helmet is reconstructed from the Welsh whetstone find, and seems to prefigure the Northumbrian Saxon Coppergate specimen from York. The javelins and the shield *umbo* are from finds on the Isle of Favret in Brittany. We have given him an expensive gold-embroidered cloak of imported silk; such quality would deserve an equally costly brooch, like the pseudo-penannular Llys Awel Farm find decorated with gilding, glass beads and amber studs. The flag bears the Christian emblems visible on Welsh stone monuments.

reconstructed from three fragments; it appears to be a one-piece shoe, with the sides raised from a now-missing sole. The heel was closed by a coarse thong, while the front seam was finely stitched, pulling the leather together in a number of folds. Across the instep there were three holes for a thong or strap.

Naturally, as in Gaul, monarchs and the wealthy nobility were resplendent in gold and purple garments (YG, XVI, LVII & CIII), gold torques and jewels. Dinogad had garments of various colours, made of the 'speckled' skins of young wolves (XC). Kenneth Dark suggests that the heavy silver chains found in north Britain represented elite insignia among the Votadini.

The study of military brooch-pins for cloaks is a scholarly discipline of its own, and space prevents any detailed description here. During the 5th century there was a gradual transition from 'crossbow' *fibulae* to pennanular types, corresponding with a revival of Celtic La Tène artistic styles. Finds in sub-Roman Britain are usually of copper alloy, sometimes with enamel inlay, but occasionally of silver. Examples dated to the 5th to 7th, and exceptionally to the 8th century, have been found across Britain from Norfolk to Wales and from Hampshire to Lincolnshire. Interpretation of brooch finds has frequently suggested cross-cultural contacts between Ireland, sub-Roman Britain, and Late Roman mainland Europe.

SELECT BIBLIOGRAPHY

Abbreviations used in text references:
AC = *Annales Cambriae;* BL = *British Library;* BM = British Museum; DEB = Gildas, *De Excidio Brettonum;* HB = Nennius, *Historia Brittonum;* HE = Bede, *Ecclesiastical History;* HF = Gregory of Tours, *Historia Francorum;* LM = London Museum; MAB = *Mabinogion ;* NMS = National Museum of Scotland; NMW = National Museum of Wales; PAS = Portable Antiquity Scheme; PDHR = Paul the Deacon, *Historia Romana;* PT = *The Poems of Taliesin;* SA = Sidonius Apollinaris: *Ep.* = *Epistulae, Pan.* = *Panegyrica;* YG = *Y Gododdin.*

ANCIENT SOURCES, including commentaries:
Almond, T.L., 'The Whitby Life of St Gregory', in *Downside Review* 23, NS 4 (1904) pp.15–29

Bede (ed King, J.E), *Opera Historica, Ecclesiastic History of the English Nation* (Cambridge, 1962)

Bede (ed & trans Colgrave, B. & Mynors, R.A.B.), *Ecclesiastical History of the English People* (Oxford, 1969)

Brett, C. (ed), *The Monks of Redon: Gesta Sanctorum Rotonensium and Vita Connuoionis* (Woodbridge, 1989)

Bromwich, R. (ed & trans), *Trioedd Ynys Prydein: The Welsh Triads* (Cardiff, 1978)

Bromwich, R., & Simon Evans, D. (eds), *Culhwch and Olwen: An Edition and Study of the Oldest Arthurian Text* (Cardiff, 1992)

Burgess, R.W., *The Chronicle of Hydatius and the Consularia Constantinopolitana: Two Contemporary Accounts of the Final Years of the Roman Empire* (Oxford University Press, 1993)

Burgess, R., 'The Gallic Chronicle of 452: A New Critical Edition with a Brief Introduction', in Mathisen R.W. & Shanzer, D. (eds), *Society and Culture in Late Antique Gaul: Revisiting the Sources* (Aldershot, 2001)

Canu Taliesin (ed Williams, I.), (Cardiff, 1960)

Cartulaire de l'Abbaye de Landevenec (ed De La Borderie, A.), (Rennes, 1888)

'Chronicle of the Princes', in *Archaeologia Cambrensis*, Vol. X, 3rd series (London, 1864)

Clancy, J. P., *Earliest Welsh Poetry* (London & New York, 1970)

Constance de Lyon (ed Borus, R.), *Vie de Saint Germain d'Auxerre* (Paris, 1965)

Cunedda, Cynan, Cadwallon, Cynddylan: Four Welsh Poems and Britain 383–655 (ed Koch J.T.), (Aberystwyth, 2013)

Eddius Stephanus (ed Colgrave, B.), *The Life of Bishop Wilfrid* (Cambridge, 1927)

Ermold le Noir, *Faites et gestes de Louis le Pieux, poeme, Annales de Saint Bertin et de Metz* (Paris, 1824)

Geoffrey of Monmouth (ed Hammer, J.) *Historia Regum Britanniae, a Variant Version Edited from Manuscripts* (Mediaeval Academy of America, 57; Cambridge, 1951)

Geoffrey of Monmouth (ed & trans Thorpe, L.), *The History of the Kings of Britain*, (Harmondsworth, 1968)

Geoffrey of Monmouth (ed Crick, J.C.), *The Historia Regum Britanniae of Geoffrey of Monmouth, III: A Summary Catalogue of the Manuscripts* (Cambridge; Brewer, 1989)

Geoffrey of Monmouth (ed & trans Thompson, A.), *The History of the Kings of Britain* (Cambridge, Ontario, 1999)

Gildas, *Opus novum. Gildas Britannus monachus, cui sapientis cognomentum est inditum, De calamitate, excidio et conquestu Britanniae, quam Angliam nunc uocant, author uetustus a multis desyderatus et nuper in gratiam d. Cuthberti Tonstalli Lond. episcopi formulis excusus* (London, 1525)

Gildas (ed Winterbottom, M.), *The Ruin of Britain and Other Works* (London & Chichester, 1978)

Giles, J.A., *The Works of Gildas and Nennius, translated from Latin, and with the former translations carefully compared and corrected* (London, 1841)

Gough-Cooper, H.W. (ed), *Annales Cambriae, the A text from British Library, Harley MS 3859, ff. 190r–193r* (Welsh Chronicle Research Group, 2015)

Gough-Cooper, H.W. (ed), *Annales Cambriae, the B text, from London, National Archives, MS E164/1, pp. 2–26* (Welsh Chronicle Research Group, 2015)

Gough-Cooper, H.W. (ed), *Annales Cambriae, the C text, from London, British Library, Cotton MS, Domitian A, i.,ff. 138r–155r* (Welsh Chronicle Research Group, 2015)

Gough-Cooper, H.W. (ed), *Annales Cambriae, the D text, from Exeter Cathedral MS 3514, pp. 523–28* (Welsh Chronicle Research Group, 2015)

Gregorio di Tours (ed Massimo Oldoni), *La Storia dei Franchi* (Milan, 1981)

Gregory of Tours (trans & intro Thorpe, L.), *Historia Francorum* (London, 1974)

Gregory of Tours (ed Van Dam, R.), *Glory of the Martyr* (Liverpool, 2004)

Haycock, M. (ed), *Legendary Poems from the Book of Taliesin* (Old College, Aberystwyth; Ceredigion, 2007)

Historical Manuscript Commission, *Report on the manuscripts in the Welsh Language,* Vol.II, part I (London, 1902)

Le Baud, P., 'Cronicques des Roys, Ducs et Princes de Bretaigne Armoricaine', in *Histoire de Bretagne avec les chroniques des maisons de Vitré et de Laval* (Paris, 1638)

The Mabinogion, Davies, S. (ed), (Oxford, 2007)

Mommsen, T. (ed), *MGH Auctores antiquissimi 9: Chronica minora saec.* IV. V. VI. VII. (I) (Berlin, 1892)

Morris, J. (ed), *British History and the Welsh Annals* (History from the Sources, 8; London & Chichester, 1980)

The Myrvyian Archaeology of Welsh, Collected out of various manuscripts; Vol. I, Poetry (London, 1901)

Nennius (trans Giles, J.A.), *History of the Britons; Historia Brittonum* (Ontario, 2000)

Notitia Dignitatum, accedunt Notitia Urbis Constantinopolitanae et laterculi Provinciarum (ed Seeck, O.), (Berlin, 1876)

Orosius (trans Fear, A.T.), *Seven Books of History against the Pagans* (Liverpool University Press, 2010)

Paolo Diacono (ed Crivellucci, A.), *Historia Romana* (Rome, 1914)

Procopius (ed Dewing, H.B.): *History of the Wars. Books VI,16–VII,15* (London, 1914 & 1992); *Books V–VI,15* (London, 1919 & 1993); *Books VII, 36–VIII* (London, 1928 & 1992)

Regino, 'Chronik', in *Quellen zur karolingischen Reichsgeschichte*, 3. Teil (Herausgegeben von Reinhold Rau, FSGA 7; Darmstadt, 1960)

Rowland, J., *Early Welsh Saga Poetry* (Cambridge, 1990)

Rutilius Namatianus (ed Malamud, M.), *Going Home – De Reditu Suo* (Routledge, 2016)

Saint Patrick (ed Hanson, R.P.C.), *Confession et letter à Coroticus* (Blanc; Paris, 1978)

Savage, A., *The Anglosaxon Chronicles, the Authentic Voices of England, from the Time of Julius Caesar to the Coronation of Henri II* (London, 2000)

Sidonius Apollinaris, in J. P. Migne, *Patrologiae Cursus Completus*, Latin Series, Vol XVIII (Paris, 1844)

Sidonius (ed Anderson, W.B.), *Poems and Letters*, II vols (Harvard University Press, 1963)

Skene, W. F. (ed), *The Four Ancient Books of Wales,* Vols I–II (Edinburgh, 1868)

The Gododdin of Aneirin (ed Koch, J.), *Text and Context from Dark Age North Britain* (Cardiff; University of Wales Press, 1997)

Vergilius Romanus, from Biblioteca Apostolica Vaticana, Cod. lat. 3867 (facsimile edition; Zurich,1985)

Wade-Evans, A.W. (ed & trans), *Vitae Sanctorum Britanniae et Genealogiae* (Cardiff, 1944)

Y Gododdin (ed & trans Williams, J.A.), A *poem on the battle of Cattraeth by Aneurin, a Welsh Bard of the Sixth Century, with an English translation and numerous historical and critical annotations* (London, 1852)

Zosimus, *Historia Nova* (London, 1814; Leipzig, Teubner, 1887)

MODERN WORKS

Akerman, J.Y., 'Second Report of Researches in a Cemetery of the Anglo-Saxon period at Brighthampton, Oxon', in *Archaeologia*, 38 (1860)

Alcock, L., *Dinas Powys: An Iron Age, Dark Age and Early Medieval Settlement in Glamorgan* (Cardiff; University of Wales Press, 1963)

Alcock, L., *Arthur's Britain: History and Archaeology AD 367–634* (London, 1971)

Alcock, L., '*By South Cadbury is that Camelot': Excavations at Cadbury Castle 1966–70* (London 1972)

Alcock, L., *Economy, Society and Warfare among the Britons and Saxons* (Cardiff, 1987)

Alcock, L., *Kings and Warriors, Craftsmen and Priests in Northern Britain, AD 550–850* (Edinburgh, 2003)

Archibald, M., Brown, M., & Webster, L., 'Heirs of Rome: the Shaping of Britain AD 400–900', in Webster, L. & Brown, M., *The Transformation of the Roman World, AD 400–900* (London, 1997)

Arnold, C. J., *Roman and Early Medieval Wales* (Stroud, 2002)

Ashe, G., *The Quest for Arthur's Britain* (Pall Mall Press, 1968)

Barford, P. M., Owen, W. G. & Britnell, W. J., 'Iron spearhead and javelin from Four Crosses, Llandysilio, Powys', in *Medieval Archaeology*, 30 (1986)

Barry, A., 'A note on the objects decorated in the Quoit Brooch Style from the burials at Saint-Marcel', in Le Boulanger, F. & Simon, L., 'La ferme antique à la nécropole de l'Antiquité tardive (milieu du Ie s. -fin du Ve s. apr. J.-C. Étude archéologique du site de Saint-Marcel le Bourg, Morbihan', in *Gallia*, 69.1 (2012)

Possible post-Roman helmet, c.800. (Private collection; photo courtesy of Artefacts)

Behmer, E., *Das zweischneidige Schwertder germanischen Völkerwanderungszeit* (Stockholm, 1939)

Birley, A., 'Brigomaglos and Riacus: a brave new world? The Balance of Power at Post-Roman Vindolanda' in Haarer, F.K. et al (eds), *AD 410: The History and Archaeology of Late and Post-Roman Britain* (Society for the Promotion of Roman Studies; London, 2014)

Breeze, A.C., 'Seventh-Century Northumbria and a Poem to Cadwallon', in *Northern History*, 38, 1 (2001)

Cardinali, M., *La Bibbia Carolingia della Abbazia di San Paolo fuori le mura* (Vatican City, 2009)

Carver, M. O. H., *The Age of Sutton Hoo: The Seventh Century in NW Europe* (Oxford; Blackwell's, 1992)

Casey, J. (ed.), *The End of Roman Britain*, BAR British Series, 71 (Oxford, 1979}

Castleden, R., *King Arthur: The Truth behind the Legend* (Routledge, 2000)

Cassard, J. C., 'La guerre des Bretons Armoricains au haut Moyen Age' in *Revue Historique*, 275 (Jan–Feb 1986)

Cassard, J. C. 'Sur le passé romain des anciens Bretons', in *Etudes sur la Bretagne et les Pays celtiques*, 5 (1996)

Chadwick Hawkes, S., 'Soldiers and settlers in Britain, Fourth to Fifth Century, with a catalogue of Animal-Ornamented Buckles and related belt-fittings', in *Medieval Archaeology*, 5, 1 (1961)

Chadwick Hawkes, S., 'The Jutish Style A: a Study of Germanic Animal Art in Southern England in the Fifth Century AD', in *Archaeologia*, 98, II (1961)

Chadwick, N., *Celtic Britain* (London, 1963)

Charles-Edwards, T. M., 'The Authenticity of the Gododdin: an Historian's View', in *Astudiaethau ar yr Hengerdd: Studies in Old Welsh Poetry* (Cardiff, 1978)

Charles-Edwards, T. M., *Wales and the Britons, 350–1064* (Oxford, 2013)

Clarkson, T., *The Men of the North; the Britons of Southern Scotland* (Edinburgh, 2010)

Cleary, S. E., *Chedworth Roman Villa* (2012)

Close-Brooks, S. & Stevenson, R.B.K., *Dark Age Sculpture* (Edinburgh, 1982)

Coleman, K., *Aspects of early medieval contact between Wales and Y Gogledd* (Newport, 2004)

Collins, R., & Allason-Jones, L. (eds), *Finds from the Frontier: Material Culture in the 4th–5th Centuries*, CBA Research Report 162 (York, 2010)

Crone, A., *The History of a Scottish Lowland Crannog: Excavations at Buiston, Ayrshire, 1989–90* (Edinburgh, 2000)

Dark, K., *Discovery by design. The identification of secular élite settlements in western Britain AD 400–700* (Oxford, 1994)

Dark, K., *Britain and the End of the Roman Empire* (Stroud 2000)

Davidson, E.H.R., *The Sword in Anglo-Saxon England: its archaeology and literature* (Woodbridge; Boydell, 1962)

Davies, S., 'The Teulu c.633–1283', in *Welsh History Review*, XXI (2003)

Davies, S., *War and Society in Medieval Wales, 633–1283* (Cardiff; University of Wales Press, 2004)

Davies, S., 'The Battle of Chester and Warfare in Post-Roman Britain', in *History, JHA* (Oxford, 2010)

Dickinson, T. M. & Härke, H., *Early Anglo-Saxon Shields*, Archaeologia Monograph 110 (1992)

Dickinson, T. M., 'Symbols of Protection: The Significance of Animal-ornamented Shields in Early Anglo-Saxon England', in *Medieval Archaeology*, 49 (2005)

Edward, J., 'Syagrius et la disparition du royaume de Soissons', in *Revue archéologique de Picardie, n°3-4. Actes des VIIIe journées internationales d'archéologie mérovingienne de Soissons, 19–22 Juin 1986* (1988)

Evans, S.S., *The Lords of Battle: Image and Reality in the 'Comitatus' in Dark-Age Britain* (Woodbridge, 1997)

Fern, C., 'The Archaeological Evidence for Equestrianism in Early Anglo-Saxon England c.450–700', in Pluskowski, A., *Just skin and bones? New Perspectives on Human-Animal relations in the Historical Past*, BAR International Series (2010)

Franckaert, B., *A putative portrayal of a 5th century centenarius from Britain*, Association Letavia (2017)

Fulton, H., *A Companion to Arthurian Literature* (Oxford; Blackwell's, 2009)

Gidlow, C., *The Reign of Arthur* (Stroud, 2013)

Giot, P. R., *Ile de Brehat, Ile Lavrec au Lavrest; Rapport scientifique sur la campagne de fouilles* (Université de Rennes, 1980)

Giot, P. R., Bernier, G., & Fleuriot, L., *Les premiers Bretons: La Bretagne du Veme siècle à l'an mil* (Bordeaux, 1988)

Glad, D., *Origine et diffusion de l'équipement défensif corporel en Méditerranée orientale (IVe-VIIIe s.). Contribution à l'étude historique et archéologique des armées historiques et médiévales* (Oxford, 2009)

Green, T., 'The British Kingdom of Lindsey', in *Cambrian Medieval Celtic Studies*, 56 (2008)

Green, T., 'Tealby, the Taifali and the end of Roman Lincolnshire' in *Lincolnshire History & Archaeology*, Vol. 46 (2011)

Green, T., *Britons and Anglo-Saxons, Lincolnshire, AD 400–600* (Lincoln, 2012)

Halsall, G., *Warfare and Society in the Barbarian West, 450–900* (London; Routledge, 2003)

Halsall, G., *Worlds of Arthur: Facts and Fictions of the Dark Ages* (Oxford, 2013)

Hamerow, H., *Excavations at Mucking Vol 2: the Anglo-Saxon Settlement, Excavations by M.U. & W.T. Jones*, English Heritage Archaeological Report 21 (London, 1993)

Heath, I., *Armies of the Dark Ages, 600–1066* (Worthing, 1980)

Hencken, H., Price, L. & Laura, E., 'Lagore Crannog: An Irish Royal Residence of the 7th to 10th Centuries AD', in *Proceedings of the Royal Irish Academy*. Section C, Vol 53 (1950/1951)

Higham, N., *King Arthur: Myth-making and History* (London; Routledge, 2002)

Hinton, D. A., *Gold and Gilt, Pots and Pins: Possessions and People in Medieval Britain* (Oxford, 2005)

Holmes, M., *King Arthur, a Military History* (Blandford, 1996)

Kantorowic, E. H., 'The Archer on the Ruthwell Cross', in *The Art Bulletin*, Vol 42, No 1 (1960)

Kazanski, M. & Vallet, F. (eds), *L'Armée romaine et les barbares du IIIe au VIIe siècle* (Paris, 1993)

Kazanski, M. & Vallet, F. (eds), *La noblesse Romaine et les chefs barbares* (Paris, 1995)

Kightly, C., *Chieftains and Princes: a Power in the land of Wales* (Cardiff, 1994)

Koch, J. T., 'Llawr en assed (*c.*932), "the laureate hero in the war-chariot": Some recollections of the Iron Age in the Gododdin', in *Etudes Celtiques,* Vol. 24 (1987)

Laycock, S., *Britannia: the Failed State, Tribal Conflicts and the End of Roman Britain* (Stroud, 2008 & 2012)

Laycock, S., *Warlords: The Struggle for Power in Post-Roman Britain* (History Press, 2011)

Le Boulanger, F., Simon, L. et al, 'De la ferme antique à la nécropole de l'Antiquité tardive [etc]: étude archéologique du site de Saint-Marcel le Bourg (Morbihan)'. in *Gallia*, 69, 1 (2012)

Lewis, M., 'La Nècropole de l'ilè Lavret, Archipel de Bréhat (Cotes-d'armor): Étude du Mobilier Médiéval', in *Bulletin de l'AMARAI*, 23 (2010)

Lyne, M., 'Late Roman Helmet fragments from Richborough', in Van Driel Murray, C., *JRMES*, 5; *Military Equipment in context*; *Proceedings of the Ninth International Roman Military Equipment Conference*, Leiden (1994)

MacGeorge, P., *Late Roman Warlords*, Oxford Classical Monographs (Oxford University Press, 2002)

Matthews, J. & Stewart, R., *Warriors of Arthur* (London, New York & Sydney, 1987)

Mersey, D., *Arthur, King of the Britons* (Chichester, 2004)

Mitchiner, M., *Jetons, Medalets and Tokens, The Medieval Period and Nuremberg*, Vol 1 (London, 1988)

Moffat, A., *Arthur and the Lost Kingdoms* (London, 1999)

Morris, J., *The Age of Arthur: a History of the British Isles from 350 to 650* (London, 1973)

Munro, R., *Ancient Scottish Lake-Dwellings or Crannogs* (Edinburgh, 1882)

Nicolle, D., *Arthur and the Anglo-Saxon Wars*, Men-at-Arms 154 (Oxford; Osprey, 1984)

Nicolle, D., *The Age of Charlemagne*, MAA 150 (Oxford; Osprey, 1984)

O'Hara, A. (ed), *Columbanus and the Peoples of Post-Roman Europe* (Oxford, 2018)

Redknap, M., *Discovered in time, Treasures from Early Wales* (Oxford; Blackwell's, 2011)

Rowland, J., 'Warfare and Horses in the Gododdin and the Problem of Catraeth', in *Cambridge Medieval Celtic Studies*, XXX (1995)

Rutherford Davis, K., *Britons and Saxons, the Chiltern Region 400–700* (Chichester, 1982)

Shadrake, D. & Shadrake, S., 'Britannia and Arthur', in *Ancient Warrior*, Vol I (Winter 1994–95)

Shadrake, D. & Shadrake, S., *Barbarian Warriors: Saxons, Vikings and Normans* (London, 1997)

Scott, J.G., 'Arms and Armour in Scotland', in *Scottish Art Review, Special No 26; Ancient Scottish Weapons* (Edinburgh, 1965)

Skene, W. F., *Arthur and the Britons in Wales and Scotland* (Felinfach; Llanerch, 1988)

Städtisches Reiss-Museum Mannheim, *Die Franken: Wegbereiter Europas vor 1500 Jahren, König Chlodwig und seine Erben* (Mainz, 1996)

Strassmeir, A., *Das Fränkische Heer der Merowingerzeit*, Teils I & II (Berlin, 2014)

Suzuki, S., *The Quoit Brooch Style and Anglo-Saxon Settlement* (Woodbridge, 2000)

Swanton, M. J., *The Spearheads of the Anglo-Saxon Settlements* (Leeds, 1973)

Thomas, C., *Tintagel: Arthur and Archaeology* (Batsford/English Heritage, 1993)

Thorpe, C., 'Incised Pictorial Slates from Tintagel', in *Cornish Studies 16, Special Issue – Tintagel Papers* (1988)

Tolley, C., 'Aethelfrith and the battle of Chester' in *Journal of the Chester Archaeological Society*, Vol 86 (2016-17)

Vermaat, R., 'The Vergilius Romanus: the first British book?', in *Vortigern Studies* (1999)

Vogt, M., *Spangenhelme* (Darmstadt, 2006)

Wagner, P., *Pictish Warrior, AD 297–841*, Warrior 50 (Oxford; Osprey, 2002)

Wainwright, G. J., *Coygan Camp, A Prehistoric, Romano-British and Dark Age settlement in Carmarthenshire* (Cardiff, 1967)

White, R. H., *Roman and Celtic Objects from Anglo-Saxon Graves;* British Archaeological Report 191 (Oxford, 1988)

White, R. H., 'Roman Material in Anglo-Saxon Graves', in *Anglo-Saxon Cemeteries: A Reappraisal* (ed Southworth, E.) (Stroud; Alan Sutton, 1990)

Wiseman, H.M., 'A British legion stationed near Orléans c. 530? Evidence for Brittonic military activity in late antique Gaul, in *Vita Sancti Dalmatii* and other sources', in *Journal of the Australian Early Medieval Association*, Vol 7 (2011)

INDEX

Page numbers in **bold** refer to illustrations and their captions.